Financing Urban and Rural Development through Betterment Levies

Jorge Macon
Jose Merino Mañon

Published in cooperation with the
Inter-American Development Bank

Financing Urban and Rural Development through Betterment Levies
The Latin American Experience

PRAEGER SPECIAL STUDIES IN INTERNATIONAL POLITICS AND GOVERNMENT

Praeger Publishers   New York   London

Library of Congress Cataloging in Publication Data

Macon, Jorge.
   Financing urban and rural development through
betterment levies.

   (Praeger special studies in international politics
and government)
   "Published in cooperation with the Inter-American
Development Bank."
   Bibliography
   Includes index.
   1. Special assessments—Latin America. 2. Latin
America—Public works—Finance. I. Mañon, José Merino
joint author. II. Inter-American Development Bank.
III. Title.
HJ4293.5.Z7M3   336.2'7   76-24359
ISBN 0-275-23970-5

PRAEGER PUBLISHERS
200 Park Avenue, New York, N.Y. 10017, U.S.A.

Published in the United States of America in 1977
by Praeger Publishers, Inc.

Printed in the United States of America

The Fifth Technical Seminar of the Inter-American Center of
Tax Administrators, held in Panama in December 1971, dealt with
a subject closely related to the process of internal resource mobilization by the public sector in Latin America: the administration of
land taxes. Under this topic, discussion centered on betterment
levies and capital gains taxes in the majority of the countries of the
region. The conclusion reached in the seminar was that the information available on this subject was inadequate for a satisfactory technical analysis of the existing systems. Based on this conclusion, the
participants in the seminar, representing 23 countries of the region,
requested that the Inter-American Development Bank finance a technical cooperation project for studying the existing experiences with
betterment levies in Latin America, and thus to obtain the technical
and scientific material required by tax authorities in the individual
countries in order to design their own instruments and operational
methodology in the field.

Since among the objectives of the Inter-American Development
Bank, as contained in its Articles of Agreement, a prominent role
is assigned to supporting the process of mobilization of internal
resources in member countries, the Bank presented the request for
consideration to its Board of Executive Directors within the framework
of the technical cooperation program and obtained authorization for
the financing of the study, which was carried out by two consultants
specialized in the field of betterment levies in member countries.
The study was made between May 1974 and May 1975. A first phase
consisted of diagnosing and analyzing past experiences and the current
situation regarding betterment levies in 11 countries selected as a
representative sample of the region. These were visited by the
consultants who authored the study. A normative model and recommendations for its implementation were prepared during a second
phase of the study on the basis of the experiences encountered in the
countries visited. During a third phase, discussions were held with
competent authorities in the countries selected regarding the feasibility of the model, recommendations and proposals for its implementation, and the socioeconomic, financial, and fiscal impact of the levy.

The Bank recognizes that the development of member countries
requires large public investments in infrastructure, the financing
of which represents an important part of budgetary outlays at different government levels. The experiences described in this study show

v

that in some countries betterment levies have come to play an important role in the amount of revenue mobilized for the financing of infrastructure projects. Although the study shows that the betterment levy is a revenue instrument requiring certain technical sophistication for its efficient application, it also indicates that, in some instances, the existence of this system has been an essential and critical factor in urban and rural development. We should also mention the positive impact of betterment levies on the rational use of land, and the increases in productivity of land generated through construction of public works—effects that discourage non-productive use and idle tenure.

This background explains the decision of the Bank to sponsor the publication of this study on betterment levies in the region in order to remedy, at least partially, the lack of systematic information on this subject. We trust that this study, with its comparative and normative orientation, will prove useful for the formulation and implementation of national policies for the financing of public works, and we also hope that the study will serve as a valuable source of information for those interested in becoming better acquainted with this matter. Within this context, the Bank is pleased to be able to support with this study the efforts of member countries, and it is grateful for the valuable cooperation that was provided to the authors of this study by tax authorities and entities related to the implementation and administration of betterment levies in the 11 countries. Furthermore, we should mention the interest of the Venezuelan authorities in this subject, manifested by an invitation to the consultants for their participation in a Seminar on Betterment Levies, sponsored by the Ministry of Finance and held at the Central Bank of Venezuela in November 1974. An additional lecture series on the subject was held in April 1975 at the Catholic University of Caracas.

The study was prepared by Jose Merino Mañon and Jorge Macon as consultants to the Inter-American Development Bank. At present, Mr. Merino is chief administrative officer of the Ministry of National Properties of Mexico (Patrimonio Nacional). Previously he was deputy director of revenue of the state of Mexico. Dr. Macon presently is professor of public finance at the National University of La Plata, and was previously director general of revenue of the province of Buenos Aires. Responsibility for the execution of this technical cooperation project in the Inter-American Development Bank was assigned to the Department of Economic and Social Development. Technical supervision was exercised by Nicholas Bruck, chief of the Financial and Special Studies Section of the General Studies Division, who relied for advice in this task on an inter-departmental working group, which included Ronald Brousseau, Gregorio del Real, Enrique Domenech, John Elac, Alfredo Gutierrez,

Jorge Lamas, Eneas Maza, and Oscar Rodriguez-Rozic. Jean-Michel Houde, economist of the Financial and Special Studies Section, collaborated in the review of the manuscript. The English translation from the Spanish original was made by Maria Carolina Bellagamba of Panama. A Spanish version of this study was published under the title Contribucion de Mejoras en America Latina by the Fondo de Cultura Economica in Mexico in the summer of 1976.

The study expresses the views of the consultants who prepared it and does not necessarily reflect the position of the Inter-American Development Bank.

CONTENTS

LIST OF TABLES

LIST OF FIGURES AND MAPS

LIST OF CHARTS

LIST OF ABBREVIATIONS

CFI   Consejo Federal de Inversiones (Federal Investment
            Council) (Argentina)

CIAT   Inter-American Center of Tax Administrators (Panama)

CIET   Centro Interamericano de Estudios Tributarios (Inter-
            American Center of Tax Studies) (Argentina)

IDB   Inter-American Development Bank (Washington, D. C.)

IMF   International Monetary Fund (Washington, D. C.)

OAS   Organization of American States (Washington, D. C.)

ONAC   Oficina Nacional de Avalúos y Catastros (National Office
            of Valuation and Land Surveys) (Ecuador)

PIDAGRO   Programa Integrado de Desarrollo Agropecuario
            (Integrated Program for Agricultural and Livestock
            Development) (Dominican Republic)

Financing Urban and Rural Development through Betterment Levies

At the Fifth Technical Seminar of the Inter-American Center of Tax Administrators (CIAT) dealing with the administration of land taxes, held in Panama City, tax officials from 23 member countries of the Inter-American Development Bank (IDB) and CIAT unanimously adopted a resolution requesting that IDB finance a technical cooperation project to study the Latin American experience with betterment levies. The purpose of this study, as expressed in the resolution, was to provide the governments of member countries with the pertinent recommendations and the technical information needed for the formulation of efficient instruments and operational procedures, permitting the public sector to recover part of the cost of public works projects through levies imposed on the increase in property values.

The resources for the financing of this project were approved by the Board of Executive Directors of the IDB on December 20, 1973, and the authors were contracted by the Bank for the execution of this study in May 1974. In obtaining authorization for the financing of the study, the Bank not only took into consideration its overall technical cooperation policies but also specifically stressed the importance of a study of this type for strengthening the mobilization of internal resources in member countries.

Before the formulation of the project, it had been assumed (and later findings confirmed the assumption) that the greatest obstacles in the implementation of betterment levy systems were technical difficulties, particularly with respect to the design of the systems for the determination of individual liabilities. This difficulty accounted for the failures of many attempts. These failures, which sometimes have only been partial, are a fact, with the notable exceptions of

Colombia and Mexico. In these two countries, the development of
the system has had significant success.

   This situation gave rise to the conclusion that it was an extremely timely occasion to undertake a study of this type, since it was
obvious that the majority of the failures were due to technical deficiencies more than to a lack of quantitative or qualitative tax policy
decisions (about which the authors are not in a position to express an
opinion). The fundamental idea sustained from the beginning was not
of formulating a study presenting abstract theory, but of making a
report with basically inductive characteristics, in other words, to
formulate standards of general application on the basis of the experiences observed, although not strictly limiting the authors to the
same.

   There is a close relationship between Chapters 2 and 4 (Conceptual Framework and Conclusions and Recommendations) and
Chapter 3 (Country Experiences). Although Chapter 4 is not a summary of the country experiences, the two chapters that precede and
follow Chapter 3 contain a general and systematic description of the
observed experiences. Only those experiences of each country that
have been deemed beneficial to other countries have been included,
and changes in guidelines have been pointed out whenever necessary.

   A study of Chapter 3, therefore, is of overriding importance
for a full understanding of the recommendations that follow it. This
implies that attention has been focused on a detailed description of
only those aspects having led either to success or failure, since they
may be used as a significant experience framework for the recovery
of property value increases through the betterment levy system when
these increases have been generated by public sector investment
projects.

   Apart from the aspects analyzed in Chapter 3 the experiences
encountered present some features that should be highlighted in this
introduction. One general comment is that the betterment levy may
be applied at all levels within the public sector, although greatest
use of the system has been made at the municipal level. There seems
to be no objection to having the levy collected by one specific level
of government even when the beneficiary is on another level. This
may even by advisable in cases when the necessary information and
technical abilities are available at a government level different from
that responsible for the public works project.

   Although this study carefully has avoided making any suggestions on the type of public works project most susceptible to financing
through the betterment levy, in order to open the door to any type of
project generating sufficiently significant value increases to justify
the cost of the administrative efforts involved in their recovery, the
examination of existing experiences indicates that both rural and

urban projects receive the same amount of attention since they both generate property value increases.

In going from a classification by sector to a classification by type of project, it may be mentioned that the betterment levy system has been used most frequently for the financing of thoroughfares and urban roads, rural roads, and sewer and drainage systems, which suggests that these public works projects are the most appropriate ones for financing through this levy. However, the authors feel that this type of consideration should not constitute a limitation to its applicability.

The experiences reviewed pertain to 11 countries. Due to different types of constraints, it was not possible to undertake a study of the situation in all IDB member countries. The 11 countries represent a sample of approximately 50 percent, which, although sufficient, cannot be considered totally comprehensive. Consequently, it is possible that other useful material for this study may exist in other countries. However, what has been examined is believed to be sufficiently comprehensive to give general validity to the conclusions with respect to the other countries also.

The criterion for the selection of the 11 countries was the assumption (not always confirmed afterward) that these countries were making the most extensive use of this type of financing.

In the opinion of the authors, the development of the Latin American countries requires large investment in public infrastructure projects, such as roads, electric energy, irrigation, and urban and rural development. The financing of these projects is an important part of public sector budgets, particularly in the case of local governments. The betterment levy can play an important role in this context, supplying the revenue that will permit the total or partial recovery of the cost of public works construction. On the other hand, the system can be an efficient instrument of resource allocation, since it puts the responsibility for payment of the costs of public works projects on the beneficiaries of the differential benefits generated by such projects, and thus the allocation of budgetary resources raised from the entire taxpayer universe will not be required.

Furthermore, when one political objective is that of improving income distribution, it is important that public infrastructure projects do not contribute, through generating increases in property values, to an increased imbalance of income and wealth levels but that, on the contrary, they contribute to a more equal distribution of wealth.

To date, the betterment levy has not been used as extensively and as frequently as appears advisable for most Latin American countries. This situation is due to difficulties regarding legal aspects, regulation, and the application of efficient administrative criteria in its implementation.

The levy is closely related to the administrative procedures followed for taxpayer registration and collection of taxes traditionally applied to real estate. However, this study is limited to an analysis of betterment levy systems in themselves. Sometimes these systems, due to a lack of a generally accepted terminology, may also be referred to in other ways.

This introduction should not close without express reference to the fact that the authors have worked with absolute intellectual freedom, without interference from the authorities of the IDB or CIAT and without any suggestions for a particular orientation. Consequently, the authors alone are responsible for each and every concept expressed in the study and none of the international agencies mentioned is in any way responsible for the ideas expressed herein.

2

**CONCEPTUAL
FRAMEWORK**

CHARACTERISTICS OF THE BETTERMENT LEVY

As most authors indicate in practically the same terms, betterment levies or special assessments are levies imposed for benefits
received, with the purpose of recovering for the public sector part
of the value of the differential benefits that are generated through the
construction of public works in the form of increases in the value of
properties. The numerous definitions in existence refer to several
additional elements, such as the requirement that the proceeds of
the levy be used to finance the same public works project on which
it is assessed; but these are elements of the definitions on which
there is less agreement. However, if the betterment levy is simply
defined as a method for the public sector to recover the "differential"
benefits generated by public works projects, the definition is narrowed
to a common denominator acceptable to most experts in the field.

To quote Edwin Seligman, perhaps the best-known writer on the
subject:

> The theory of the betterment charge or assessment
> according to benefits is very simple. It rests upon the
> almost axiomatic principle that if the government by
> some positive action confers upon an individual a
> particular measurable advantage, it is only fair to the
> community that he should pay for it. The facts may be
> in question, for it may happen that the particular advan-
> tage is only ostensible, or that the special benefit is
> not measurable. But the facts being given, the principle
> seems self-evident.[1]

5

The betterment levy is a compulsory assessment, which means that it is compulsory, and its compulsory nature distinguishes it from fees or rates for public services. (It should be recalled that in conventional terminology, revenues refer to all compulsory public-revenue-raising measures, whereas a tax is a type of charge not associated with any specific service and a fee is a charge associated with a particular service.) It is not a tax because it is linked to a specific benefit received, nor is it a fee since it is not tied to a service. In the conventional classification of public revenues, therefore, a special category had to be established to permit the inclusion of betterment levies.

The tax policy standards governing the betterment levy are based on the benefit principle; in other words, the levy burden is imposed on taxpayers in accordance with the benefits generated by public sector activities. In this case, instead of a service, there is a potential or anticipated increase in property value. [2]

The purpose of the betterment levy is to recover for the public sector the (special) differential benefits caused by public works and derived by landowners in the form of increases in the value of property. There may be a case of heterodoxy here, since many writers refer to "differential" or "special" benefits rather than to "increases in the value of property" or "value increases." However, a close examination of this point reveals that the increase in value resulting from a public works project simply consists of the differential benefits expected from the project, capitalized at the shadow rate of interest. (The term "shadow rate of interest" is used to denote the opportunity cost of capital, that is the yield that would be obtained from its most productive alternative use.) This statement, while it might seem of mere academic interest, is, however, a necessary refinement of definition since the term "increase in value," while for practical effect amounting to the same thing as "differential benefit," is much more specific and measurable. [3]

The scope of the term "differential benefit" is different from that of "general benefit." A public works project primarily yields a general benefit to the entire community or to a broad sector of the community. This is the objective normally sought when the project is at the planning stage. But it also yields (special) differential benefits in that some people benefit more than others as a result of different circumstances, often derived from the physical proximity of their properties to the project. The system of betterment levies examined here is aimed at recovering for the public sector only the latter type of benefit.

It should be stressed that it is not necessary for such differential benefits to exist in actual fact; their potential existence is enough for their capitalization in the form of value increases.

The (special) differential benefits or increases in property values are those directly generated by the construction of a public works project. They exclude increases in value caused by the general growth of the community or by a rise in the general price level. In other words, the betterment levy is neither imposed on the increase in the total value of property nor on relative increases in the value of real property as compared to other assets. It is only imposed on the increase in the value of real property resulting from a public works project in relation to the increase in value of other real properties not benefiting from the project.

In some countries, for example, Argentina, it has been found that some projects are financed by landowners associations or by cost-sharing arrangements. They usually involve paving less important streets, which added together represent substantial amounts of investments. This system, which is sometimes mistaken for the betterment levy and even wrongly known as such, consists of an association of landowners who jointly finance paving costs in proportion to the frontage of their parcels on the improved street.

Sometimes this kind of collective project financing is not provided for under tax legislation and, as is the case in Brazil, its legal framework falls within the realm of private law, which implies that a unanimous agreement of all frontage landowners is required for the project to be carried out. In other cases, for example, Ecuador's municipalities, cost-sharing projects are provided for under tax legislation as compulsory charges, and the responsibility for selecting and implementing public works projects falls entirely onto government entities, prior consultation with potential beneficiaries not being required. This type of situation bears a closer resemblance to the betterment levy system.

However, despite its compulsory character, there is a conceptual difference from the betterment levy. Cost-sharing projects are focused on works jointly undertaken, while in the betterment levy system the tax obligation is not generated by the joint undertaking but by the increase in the value of property resulting from the public works project.

Thus, while in joint projects each landowner pays in proportion to his frontage and practically defrays the cost of a given amount of paved square meters, in the betterment levy system, two landowners with the same frontage may pay different charges if one parcel is more valuable than the other (for reasons of shape or topography of the lots), since it may be anticipated that the higher the preproject value of the property, the greater the increase in value resulting from the public works project.

This distinction becomes clear when consideration goes from the paving of side streets to large-scale projects, where the incremental impact not only has an incidence on frontage parcel owners but also reaches parcels located in intersecting and parallel streets.

The imposition of a betterment levy on the increased value of property capitalized as a result of differential benefits generated by public works inevitably leads to consideration of compensation for decreases in land value resulting from the capitalized value of the differential damages generated by public works projects.

There are many instances in which a public works project not only generates benefit for the community and differential benefits (betterments) for some landowners but also some "worsements." For example, changing an urban traffic artery into a one-way rapid transit thoroughfare can damage greatly the business of the stores adjoining it; replacement of an ordinary road by an expressway can put gasoline stations already located on the road out of business; construction of a garbage incinerator decreases the value of adjoining properties; and so on.

It is clear that, if the same logic that justifies the betterment levy is used, these types of cases merit a "compensation for worsement," that is, a subsidy or credit. Yet, with the exception of Panama, no such provisions exist in any of the legislations examined, although compensations may be obtained through court action based on common law.

There is, however, one type of compensation for which legal provision is made in practically all countries examined. This compensation is not made because of a decrease in the value of property resulting from public works projects but because of total or partial physical use of a parcel for a public project. These are what are know as the expropriations frequently required to obtain the spatial layout necessary for a public works project.

The practice of compensation for condemnation (the state's exercise of its power of eminent domain) has become discredited because of payments made by the public sector that are below the actual value of property, a circumstance that accounts for organized opposition to public works projects on the part of landowners threatened with expropriation. Consequently, some countries, for example, Colombia, prefer to negotiate the purchase of the properties required or to expropriate them at an equitable price. Although more costly to the public sector, this system usually facilitates the construction of public projects, and is just as equitable as the betterment levy itself.

Reference already has been made to the importance of the betterment levy within a framework of real property taxation, as concerns the financing of urban development projects[4] and programs

to increase rural productivity in areas where public works generate
differential benefits leading to increases in the value of property.

ROLE OF THE BETTERMENT LEVY IN
INCOME DISTRIBUTION AND RESOURCE ALLOCATION

Purchase of land without an immediate development target in
mind is, in the first place, a hedge against inflation. Land is particularly suitable for this purpose, in spite of its low liquidity. Second,
investors expect an increase in prices of land, as compared to other
assets, due to urban growth and the general development of the
community. Finally, speculators often anticipate increases in the
relative prices of certain parcels as compared to other real property,
stemming from the construction of public projects that may increase
the value of those properties. Thus, it is clear that construction of
public works has a secondary effect, that of increasing the net
worth of landowners.

It is logical to assume that speculative investments of this type
are made by high-income individuals and it follows that a secondary
effect of the construction of public works projects, from the standpoint of income distribution, is a further concentration of income.
Thus, the betterment levy, if properly designed to offset the increases
in land values it generates, becomes a useful instrument for countries
wishing to avoid a worsening of income distribution. If properly
enacted and enforced, betterment levies either discourage land
speculation stemming from anticipation of public works or recover
the increase in value for the public sector.

In this context, betterment levies become instruments that,
although not contributing to an improved income distribution, do
avoid further income disparity. It must be added, however, that
this impact is relatively small, due to the secondary importance of
betterment levies as sources of public revenues as compared with
primary sources, such as the income tax. Furthermore, the external benefits which it is expected that public works will yield, encourage speculative investment in land, often only in anticipation of the
possibility of an increase in the future price of land through the construction of public works.

Land speculation channels savings toward the purchase of rural
or urban land, in other words, toward existing natural resources that,
in principle, are not intended for productive use and thereby reduce
effective demand for new goods or capital goods capable of producing
other goods and services. This does not mean that the flow of savings
to land purchases is totally undesirable, since land is also a factor

of production; however, it is clear that, whenever public works enhance land value, the danger of a speculative misallocation of savings from more to less productive investment is present.

Speculation, although sometimes monopolistic, may play a positive role in a market economy through contributing to greater price stability, ensuring a regular flow of goods to the market. However, speculation in natural resources, such as land, may contribute to unreasonably high prices, be detrimental to productive use of land and contribute to unreasonably high land prices.

COMPARISON OF BETTERMENT LEVIES
AND OTHER FISCAL INSTRUMENTS
WITHIN THE TAX SYSTEM

Public works projects normally pursue well-defined objectives, that is, to provide such specific services as transportation networks, irrigation of agricultural land, draining of flood areas, sewer systems, and so on. But normally these projects are not explicitly aimed at increasing the value of parcels functionally linked, so that such value increases are not ordinarily a major objective of public works projects. Consequently, in the absence of a betterment levy system, it is usual for projects financed with public funds to lead to gains for specific groups at the cost of all taxpayers. Thus, the function of the betterment levy, within the tax system, is to recover these external benefits generated by public works projects, thereby reducing the overall tax burden of the community.

However, failure to understand fully the scope of the betterment levy has led some persons, sometimes government officials, to underestimate its importance as a source of project financing on grounds that other instruments fulfill a similar function without the additional administrative cost implied by this levy. Three alternative instruments are mentioned in this respect: user taxes, tariffs, and fees; capital gains taxes; and real estate taxes. As the following discussion shows, these fiscal instruments usually have quite different functions and cannot be considered as substitutes for the betterment levy.

User Taxes, Tariffs, and Fees

User taxes such as gasoline taxes to finance road construction, commonly used in many countries, represent a general application of the benefit principle, since motorists are charged indirectly for road construction and maintenance costs. Yet the role of a user tax differs from that of a betterment levy even though both fiscal instruments finance the construction of public works and are based on the benefit principle. A motorist may or may not own land adjacent to the road. If he is not a property owner, his share in the cost of the road which corresponds to the benefits he receives could be imposed on him only through the user tax. If, on the other hand, he is an owner of property adjacent to the road, the user tax will only rarely approach a sum proportional to the increase in value his property has experienced.

Consequently, a user tax and a betterment levy have different, functions, so that their coexistence is justified. The user tax attempts to allocate the external cost of benefits conferred to motorists by the road, while the betterment levy's objective is to recover part of the increase in value generated by the road construction.

Public works are frequently financed by periodically collected service charges and overhead charges covering construction or installation overhead expenses. One example is the financing system of water supply facilities in villages located in Argentina's Mendoza Province. This procedure differs from the betterment levy in that the latter is a one-time charge, whereas overhead surcharges are imposed periodically either on a permanent basis or at least for a long period of time. However, this distinction is more apparent than real since both payment flows either can be discounted or capitalized to find comparable present valuations; the distinction between a betterment levy and a recurrent surcharge, then, becomes one of form rather than substance.

These surchanges, however, do not necessarily play the same role as the betterment levy. The similarity holds in some cases, while in others it does not. This can be seen in an examination of the three cases mentioned, all of which represent examples deliberately chosen: tolls, irrigation fees and construction surcharges, and charges for the installation and use of sewers.

Although more precise than a user tax in the distribution of the tax burden of road construction, highway tolls perform basically the same function. Highway tolls distribute the costs of road construction and maintenance to motorists in a way fairly similar to, although more efficient than, a user tax. They cannot, therefore, have the same function as a betterment levy, since the benefits derived by the motorists in using a road have no relation to the property value increases benefiting the owners of adjacent land.

Irrigation fees and construction surcharges are another example. Assuming that, because of an irrigation project, land values increase in proportion to the volume of water supplied to each lot, and that irrigation fees are based on water consumption, if individual construction surcharges are a fixed share of irrigation fees, they will be proportional to the corresponding land value increments.

If the surcharge paid by any user is, when capitalized at the shadow interest rate, equal to the value increase accruing to his lot, it will be exactly equivalent to a betterment levy, which recovers the entire differential benefit. However, the extent of land appreciation need not be proportional to the volume of water supplied, as would occur if the productivity of land were not uniform across the lots. Thus, the surcharge and the betterment levy frequently have a different fiscal incidence.

A similar situation arises with regard to charges raised for the installation of sewer systems. If operating fees are set in proportion to current or potential use of the sewer, they may also be proportional to property value increases (assuming that rates of installation surcharges also are proportional to the same value increases). Consequently, if the present value of recurring surcharges, discounted when temporary and capitalized when permanent, is equal to the corresponding property appreciation, it should be equivalent to 100 percent of the betterment levy.

Capital Gains Tax

It is sometimes argued that the addition of a betterment levy becomes redundant when capital gains taxes are imposed on the value increments of real estate. (Note that capital gains tax is also known as land value increase tax when only imposed on real property.) There are, however, basic differences between the two.

First, capital gains derived from real estate holdings are taxable only at the time of sale, and such transactions may be infrequent or may never take place. Second, the major purpose of the capital gains tax is not to tax property value increases, per se, although the tax does also have this effect. The purpose of the capital gains tax in general is to complement the income tax. It taxes capital gains realized over many years in one particular year at a fixed rate since the application of the progressive income tax rates could generate an excessive tax liability during one particular year. This is evidenced by the coverage of the capital gains tax, which includes not only land and real estate but also all other assets that generate capital gains when they are sold, although these gains actually may have been generated in previous years.

Third, the capital gains tax is levied on the entire gain realized at the time of sale. This includes (in absence of monetary correction) the increase in real estate values resulting from a general increase in the price level, the increase in the relative price of real estate as compared to that of other forms of wealth, and the appreciation of particular real estate holdings relative to other similar holdings.

In contrast, the betterment levy is applicable only to the last item insofar as the relative appreciation is attributable to a public works project.

Another difference between the capital gains tax and the betterment levy relates to their respective rates as found in actual applications. Whereas in the case of a betterment levy, rates on the order of 50 to 100 percent are the rule, the capital gains tax rate may not exceed 25 percent.

Although there is some overlapping in the incidence of the two preceding fiscal tools, in practice this problem can be corrected if the amount of the betterment levy is deducted when calculating the capital gains tax liability.

Real Estate Tax

Finally, real estate or real property tax is considered. The fact that betterment levies and real estate taxes have a similar tax base gives some support to the view that the introduction of a betterment levy may be superfluous. The underlying rationale holds that differential benefits accruing to property owners from public works projects are already covered under the real estate tax and need not be taxed a second time.

Leaving aside the problems of the timely registration of real estate appreciation in public records, various objections to the preceding viewpoint can be raised.

One objection comes from the rates of taxation. Whereas property tax rates are normally small, frequently below 1 percent and rarely higher than 2 percent, betterment levies for the most part fluctuate as already noted, between 50 and 100 percent (see Chapter 3). Even though the property tax is levied annually, whereas the betterment tax is a one-time liability, and even making the comparison on an appropriate basis, there still remains a very large difference.

To make the effects of the two similar would require that the rate of the property tax be set equal to the shadow rate of interest for the betterment levy. For example, with a shadow rate of 10 percent, a 7 percent annual real estate tax would have the same fiscal incidence as a 70 percent betterment levy. However, the rate of 7 percent is in fact well above prevailing real estate tax rates.

But there is a more important objection. Assume that to recover the differential value increments generated by a betterment project, a 7 percent real estate tax is imposed annually on property owners. While this rate may be appropriate to recover the differential benefits received by properties within the benefit area, it would

be excessive if imposed also on other properties that do not receive
such a benefit. In other words, taxing betterments generated by
public authority and those generated by the owner himself with the
same rate represents a visible lack of equity.

THE CONDEMNATION OF PROPERTY

The increases in real estate values generated by public works
projects at times may have such magnitude that they represent the
major portion of the increase in value the property has experienced.
This situation is found in various types of public works projects, but,
as Alberto Lukszan pointed out to the authors, it is most obvious in
the case of irrigation projects, which can convert deserts into
fertile land.

Imposing a betterment levy based on post-betterment property
values would give rise to sizable fiscal liabilities on property owners,
many of whom would be unable to meet this financial obligation. A
more expedient course of action probably would be to condemn and
expropriate the properties in question and subsequently sell them at
public auction. This alternative may be preferable because expropriation entails little cost to the public sector except for the price paid
for the land and circumvents the difficulty of collecting sizable levies
from property owners. In addition, the auction of irrigated land may
improve its allocation to more productive farmers.

LIMITATIONS OF SIMPLE
DETERMINATION PROCEDURES

In various cases, betterment legislation has a tendency to
establish simplified procedures for the determination of liabilities
of each property owner, which is sometimes necessary because of a
lack of information from the cadastre, or on occasion it aims to reduce administrative costs or to obviate problems of design.

While such operational simplifications may help decrease costs
of design and administration, and may even be necessary, they also
lead to a weakening of the betterment levy as an instrument for project financing. Consequently, the combination of oversimplified levy-
determination rules and inaccurate measurement of property value
increases may result in levy-benefit ratios that vary greatly among
property owners. One of two distortions may occur: either the betterment levy is, in the aggregate, too high and imposes an excessive
burden on the property owners at the lower end of the benefit scale
or the level of betterment levy financing is too low and thus exempts

part of the value increase accruing to the most-favored beneficiaries from making an appropriate contribution.

While the first situation may lead to organized opposition on the part of property owners, the second may undermine the financial base of the betterment project and prevent or delay its implementation.

In this regard, the general historic evolution of taxation provides some useful insights. In the past, when only low levels of taxation were necessary, taxes could be simple and rudimentary because gross inequities were not very important, because of the low level of taxation. However, as the need for government revenues increased, new forms of taxation were introduced (such as income taxes) that define the tax base in a more flexible way and require the use of deductions with the objective of mitigating gross fiscal inequities that, with progressive rates, otherwise could have serious consequences.

The betterment levy presents a somewhat similar situation: relatively simple and unsophisticated assessment rules may only generate low revenue yields and thus weaken the system as a source for project financing.

In this manner, equity, which is in our countries based on generally accepted principles of justice, also has the effect of generating more public revenue for (often very necessary) public works, since the use of the equity principle requires a more sophisticated system resulting in higher levy quotas. For example, some betterment levy legislations, in the absence of reliable cadastral records, determine individual liabilities on the basis of such physical units of measurement as road frontage, square meters of surface area, and so on.

This procedure overlooks the fact that the more valuable properties have a greater increase in value increments than those of lesser value. In fact, one can expect a certain degree of proportionality between original property values and post-betterment values. Without a detailed record of real estate property values, it will be necessary to establish the levy for value increases at the level of the least benefited. This can provide an acceptable basis for determination of liabilities, but, as a result, part of the differential benefits going to the most valuable properties remains untaxed and the levy as a source of finance will lose importance.

This problem has been recognized in the legislation of some countries. In Colombia, for example, instead of assessment records weighting factors of physical measurements are used that partly serve as proxies for property values. Frequently overlooked in the apportionment of betterment levies within a specific benefit area is the fact that some subareas receive greater benefits than others. A more equitable prorating of betterment levies requires the use of operational indexes capable of depicting locational differences and the assessment of recoverable value increments accordingly. The Colombian system provides such an example. As indicated above, the financial importance of the betterment levy for project financing can be enhanced through a relatively small effort aimed at constructing adequate parameters.

Therefore, cost-saving assessment procedures that may seem to be a desirable goal can turn out to be a factor that reduces the revenue raising of the betterment levy. However, there is a need to reach a compromise between simplicity and revenue capacity. This trade-off between administrative expediency and revenue capacity needs to be weighted in light of the circumstances of each specific case.

ASSESSED VALUES AS A
BASIS FOR LEVY DETERMINATION

This study of the experiences of 11 Latin American countries reveals that the availability of cadastral assessment records is not essential to an effective implementation of a betterment levy system and that it can be applied, still at a reasonable cost, in the absence of a cadastre. Needless to say, however, a well-designed cadastral system facilitates assessment procedures a great deal and reduces operation costs.

A cadastral system may be divided into three separate components corresponding to a frequently used classification of cadastral systems on the basis of their physical, legal, and fiscal characteristics. [5] These three components will now be evaluated from the standpoint of betterment levy implementation.

The physical cadastre is a public registry of maps and surveys recording the location and size of properties along with other physical features, such as topography, boundaries, roads, productive use, and so forth. The more developed the cadastre is, the more complete the details of the physical characteristics of a given area.

The usefulness of a physical cadastre for the implementation of a betterment levy is fairly obvious. It serves to identify the properties subject to the levy and to determine the functional link of each property to the public works project to be financed; the link determines the increase in property value. Where a physical cadastre is not available, a limited physical survey has to be made, although a cadastre intended solely for the purposes of the betterment levy need not be extremely detailed or accurate. As will be discussed later, a record of such information may be useful in the absence of a fiscal cadastre.

An examination of the availability of this type of information in Latin America reveals a fairly acceptable situation. In some countries, the development of cadastral records is now underway, and while incomplete in many areas, these records already cover a fairly large percentage of their territories, particularly the more densely populated areas where the probability for betterment levy financing is highest.

The legal cadastre is essentially a system of identifying ownership and real estate rights and other relevant property law. The legal cadastre may serve to identify persons liable for betterment levies in a given area and provide the basis for initiating court action whenever necessary.

With few exceptions, the legal cadastres of the 11 countries studied were not kept up to date. Although public information of ownership transfers and other property transactions is generally available, administrative backlogs frequently delay its timely integration into the records of the cadastre. In some instances, legal cadastres even have been abandoned because of excessive processing time lags.

When lacking a reliable legal registry, it is possible to implement a betterment levy, although at greater costs, by the use of the administrative system established for the collection of property taxes: tax liabilities are imposed on properties without identifying their respective owners. However, the anonymity of beneficiaries precludes direct collection of levies from the owners' residences or settlement of defaulting payments through personal contacts made by tax administration officials. Moreover, there is the difficulty of taking legal action against unidentified persons (when so authorized) in the hope that property owners reveal their identity. Due to possible legal complications and administrative lags, particularly in cases of noncompliance, this alternative method entails considerably larger operational costs.

Finally, the fiscal cadastre is a record of property values assigned to real estate holdings on the basis of their value components, for example, land, residential, or industrial structures and other forms of private real estate.

The usefulness of a fiscal cadastre for the application of a betterment levy is that the assessed values it contains can become the basis for prorating all or part of the cost of a public works project. The apportionment of project costs to individual property owners depends on the weights attached to the parameters selected as proxy indicators of property values and on the fiscal incidence of betterment levies imposed on estimated value increases. The assumption that value increases are proportional to original property values, or to a related index such as physical dimensions, remains valid even if this proportionality is partially changed through appropriate parameters.

A central requirement generally placed upon property valuation of fiscal cadastres is that it be commensurate with market values. Unfortunately, because market values of properties are continually rising, this requirement represents a serious difficulty for countries subject to persisting inflation. In fact, the only necessary requirement that fiscal cadastres must fulfill to be a reliable basis for betterment levy prorating is that they be equal to a fixed proportion of market values. The ratio of cadastral to market values may be 0.05, 0.50, 0.80, or even above unity (that is, the cadastral values may be 5 percent, 50 percent, or 80 percent of market values or may even exceed them), provided the ratio is constant in every case.

To illustrate the importance of this requirement, assume that two properties with equal market values receive equal benefits from a public works project, but that one of them is assessed at 50 percent of its market value and the other at 5 percent. Clearly, prorating on the basis of assessed values will result in the first owner paying a betterment levy 10 times as large as the second. Since this would violate the fiscal principle of horizontal equity, the betterment levy would have to remain small in order to avoid the serious fiscal disparities that would result from a high level of imposition when applied to differing assessments.

The overall picture found in the examined Latin American cadastral systems is one of great variance of cadastral-market value ratios. Ratio dispersions as vast as 5 to 50 percent, just cited as an illustration, are quite common and ratio dispersions between the extremes of 5 percent and 80 percent were also found. The basic reason for this is that countries experiencing inflationary spirals make partial property revaluations either when property is revaluated because of the property sale or construction or when systematic revaluations are made by tax administrators for specific zones or areas and the new values are assessed on the basis of the prices prevailing at the time of revaluation. As a result, these countries do not have reliable fiscal cadastres because the values are not based on sets of comparable prices.

Exceptions are found in countries with low inflation, such as Ecuador, or with a long tradition of inflation, such as Argentina, where tax administrators often have decided to regularly adjust property assessments on the basis of constant prices of a base period. Consequently, apart from distortions in relative prices, the fiscal registries of these countries are based on cadastral-market value coefficients with an acceptable degree of consistency.

There are two circumstances when these limitations of fiscal cadastres become less important. First, the requirement of a

constant ratio between cadastral and market property values is only
applicable to the area subject to the betterment levy. The fact that
value ratios are dispersed across a country or a region does not
necessarily imply that they are not homogeneous within a given area.
Second, the value components usually most affected by cadastral-
market value disparities are attributable to construction and other
private accessions to property, so that greater homogenity can be
expected by prorating a betterment levy solely on the basis of land
values.

It is evident that to facilitate the introduction of a betterment
levy system, a serious attempt to establish and maintain reliable
fiscal cadastres is necessary. Nevertheless, the Colombian experience shows that it is possible to implement an adequate betterment
levy without incurring excessive operational costs when a reliable
fiscal cadastre does not exist (see the case study on Colombia in
Chapter 3).

GENERAL DESCRIPTION OF A
STANDARD ASSESSMENT PROCEDURE

Empirical evidence (described in greater detail in Chapter 3)
shows that it is useful to divide the process of betterment levy determination into three stages: determination of the benefit area, determination of the aggregate benefit, and determination of levies to be
imposed on each beneficiary.

Determination of the Benefit Area

The first task involved in the standard procedure is to determine
the area receiving the benefit from the public works project, which is
equivalent to identifying the property owners subject to the betterment
levy. This is generally done through the study of physical maps
showing property boundaries, streets, topography, cadastral codes,
and other details necessary to establish the nature and limits of the
benefit area.

The nature and size of the benefit area will vary according to
the type of public works project. Sometimes the area can be determined very precisely. For example, for an irrigation project, it is
the area of land irrigated; for a sewer system, the area served; for
a drainage network, the surface drained; and so on. In other cases,
the benefit area may be determined less by the nature of the project
itself than by related physical conditions. An example is the paving
of urban streets where such factors as physical obstacles, major

roads, or railroads often may delimit the benefit area. A similar situation arises with the paving of rural roads, where the benefit area is frequently delimited by topographic features. Where such limits do not exist and the differential benefits of a public works project have indefinite spatial boundaries, it becomes necessary to select a cutoff point in the light of concrete considerations related to the betterment project.

In some cases, it may be preferable to select initially a large benefit area to avoid the possibility of excluding some differential beneficiaries and, subsequently, after the benefits received by each individual property are assessed, to exempt those properties where the benefits are negligible or below a minimum level.

Determination of the Aggregate Benefit

Once the benefit area is determined, it is necessary to estimate the aggregate benefit received by that area in terms of increases in property values. Evidence shows that it is common practice to use the services of real estate appraisers, who estimate the benefits of a small sample of properties suitably distributed across the benefit area. The aggregate amount of benefit in money terms then can be interpolated to all the remaining properties on the basis of the information contained in the survey map. This information, collected before the public works project is started, is used to inform the authorities of the project's capacity to mobilize revenues through betterment levies in terms of a percent of the aggregate cost of the project.

A rather obvious recommendation, particularly in the early stages of a country's experience with the betterment levy, is that the proportion of the cost of the project that is to be financed with betterment levies should be significantly below the total estimated value of benefits in order to minimize the effects of administrative errors detrimental to the beneficiaries and to avoid damaging public confidence in the system.

Determination of the Levy to Be Imposed on Each Beneficiary

After defining the benefit area and the percentage of the aggregate cost of the project that can be recovered through the levy on the increase in property values, the next step is to prorate this sum among the properties included in the benefit area.

The most important point to be analyzed is the nature of the variables that will serve as the basis for prorating. Obviously, the most suitable variable is the actual benefit received by each property, expressed in terms of money values of property appreciation. Thus, the levy can be imposed on the increase in values at a uniform rate equal to the ratio between the amount to be captured and the aggregate of value increases.

Existing evidence indicates, however, that given the available administrative and technical capabilities, the direct estimation of increases in values and benefits is difficult and very costly. A practical solution to this difficulty is to estimate benefits through the use of magnitudes that in some way will be acceptable substitutes.

As a first approximation, total charges could be prorated on the basis of property values prior to construction of the public works project (pre-project values). This operation would be symbolized as follows:

$$C_i = \frac{K \quad V_i}{\sum V_i}$$

where C_i is the betterment levy quota to be imposed on property i, K is the amount to be financed, and V_i is the value of property i.

This method implies that the benefits are considered to be proportional to pre-project values. In analytic terms, this means that the functional relationship between the pre-project value and the value increment has a positive derivative, that is, the greater the pre-project value of the property, the greater the value appreciation.

However, this does not mean that the proportion is constant, that all properties experience an equal relative increase in value. In analytic terms, although the function has a positive derivative, it is not linear. Linear proportionality, however, can be roughly the case with respect to certain types of public works projects, such as the construction of a sewer system, for which it can be expected that each property will benefit approximately in proportion to its value, the functional link with the project being the same for all properties.

This will not necessarily be true, however, in most other cases in which other factors will come into play in addition to the value of the properties prior to the public works construction (which, in the case of rural properties, also indicate their productivity). An example is the benefit accruing to a property as a result of a thoroughfare. The benefits generated by an irrigation project will depend on the amount of irrigation water each property can receive. The benefits derived by each property from the construction of a highway,

however, will depend on its distance from the highway, and the
benefits of a drainage system will be greater for properties at lower
elevations and smaller for properties at higher elevations.

Thus, there is a need for the use of factors that permit the
measurement of the relative weight of the values for the purpose of
determining the levy according to the benefits received. The burden
of the levy then will fall more heavily on the properties receiving
greater benefits and more lightly on the others. Algebraically
expressed,

$$C_i = \frac{K \,(B_1 \, B_2 \, \ldots \, B_j \, \ldots \, B_n) \, _i \, V_i}{\sum (B_1 \, B_2 \, \ldots \, B_j \, \ldots \, B_n) \, _i \, V_i}$$

where B_j represents the benefit factors. The nature of the benefit
factors can be highly diverse and, to a large extent, depends on the
problems generated by factual circumstances arising in each case,
which, as stated earlier, are extremely varied. (The various
situations with respect to benefit factors are discussed in the case
studies of Colombia and Mexico in Chapter 3.)

The prorating system described above assumes that the basic
apportionment variable is the value of the properties. This, in turn,
assumes that adequate information is available, that is, a fiscal
cadastre exists that meets the requirement (at least in the area
affected by the project) that the assessed values recorded are in a
constant ratio to market values.

The condition of a constant ratio of cadastral-market values
usually is not satisfied, particularly in countries that have experienced inflation for a number of years. These countries only make
partial property revaluations, at the price level applicable to different periods, so that their fiscal cadastres show assessed values that
correspond to different time periods and do not satisfy the condition
of constant cadastral-market values ratio.

In such cases, it is appropriate to use as a basic magnitude for
the determination of the levy the physical surface area of each property, which is generally found in physical cadastres. The latter are
more commonly available than fiscal cadastres containing the information described above. Moreover, where physical cadastres are
lacking, the information can be obtained by means of a limited physical survey.

However, this physical magnitude lacks some of the merits of
the money values, since not only the unit value of land but also the
incremental values can vary widely from one property to the next.
In the absence of satisfactory constant values, a new set of indexes
has to be added, which here are called value indicators, and which

are reflected in the following equation that completes the equation given previously:

$$C_i = \frac{K(B_1 B_2 \ldots B_j \ldots B_n)_i (V_1 V_2 \ldots V_j \ldots V_n)_i \, a_i}{\sum (B_1 B_2 \ldots B_j \ldots B_n)_i (V_1 V_2 \ldots V_j \ldots V_n)_i \, a_i}$$

where V_j represents the value factors and a_i represents the physical area of property i.

These value indicators normally are based on factual circumstances. (Some of the value indicators are also reviewed under the experiences of Colombia and Mexico in Chapter 3.) It should be pointed out, however, that these indicators are often reflected in property assessment systems, such as topography, configuration of the land, location, and so on. Since assessment systems differ from country to country because of differences in climate, topography, local customs, and economic systems, the factors included in this group will depend on the particular situation of each country.

Finally, it may be necessary to use additional factors of a different nature. For example, factors may have to be applied that reduce the tax liability (perhaps even to zero) for lower income groups or raise it for higher income groups, applying the principle of ability to pay or pursuing the objective of improving income distribution. Another possibility that also implies the application of the principle of ability to pay is graduation of the levy, increasing it for land on which buildings have been erected or in accordance with its economic use. Many considerations can come into play regarding this group of miscellaneous factors, depending principally on the nature of the tax system, local customs in the country concerned, and the prevailing opinions in the sectors affected (see Chapter 3).

The final result of this combination of indicators can be expressed with the following equation:

$$C_i = \frac{K(B_1 B_2 \ldots B_j \ldots B_n)_i (V_1 V_2 \ldots V_n)_i (M_1 M_2 \ldots M_j \ldots M_n)_i \, a_i}{\sum (B_1 B_2 \ldots B_j \ldots B_n)_i (V_1 V_2 \ldots V_j \ldots V_n)_i (M_1 M_2 \ldots M_j \ldots M_n)_i \, a_i}$$

where M_j represents the miscellaneous indicators.

Determination of Value Factors

A problem common to all these value factors is how they are to be quantified. Two schools of thought exist in this respect. One recommends that indicators be determined objectively, as a function of a specific variable, and the other that they be determined subjectively. In reality, neither of these positions can be taken as conclusive. The advocates of the first approach agree that some of the indicators cannot be determined objectively, while the advocates of the second position agree that some of them can, in fact, be determined objectively. Choice of either method implies no more than a preference for one or the other, as some of the indicators can be determined by either method.

The objective method offers the advantage of lower administrative costs. It actually only requires a prior investigation to determine the indicators on the basis of a given variable. An example is the paving of an urban thoroughfare where it could be established that the indicator will be inversely proportional to the shortest distance to the thoroughfare via existing roads. In other words, the function relating the indicator to distance will have a negative derivative.

However, this does not mean that the indicator necessarily will have to be inversely proportional to distance in numerical terms, since this could lead to absurd solutions. An example is an excellent quantitative study made for the Caracas metropolitan subway project in which the factor was made inversely proportional to walking distance (in minutes) from the property to the nearest station. The method led to results that concentrated the betterment levy on areas closer to the station, while having a light incidence on areas more distant to the same, as compared to what a subjective judgment of vertical equity would have shown to be desirable. This was the reason underlying the need for more complex inverse ratios in the Caracas project. [6]

However, an advocate of the subjective method would argue that the search for analytic expressions providing results consistent with a given concept of vertical equity is clearly no less subjective than a direct selection of parameters. In fact, there is very little difference between selecting an equation offering the results sought and directly stating those results in quantitative terms.

It is also clear, as stated by advocates of the objective method, that this method, after having been properly tested, acts as a safeguard against the possibility of individual mistakes.

There is little value in the argument that, by working out a formula for determination of factors, a practical determination of these factors can be left to less skilled personnel. When subjective methods are used, the indicators can be determined on the basis of a few sample properties, leaving determination of the remainder to less skilled personnel on the basis of previously worked-out interpolation methods.

Nor can much importance be attached to the fact that these methods may be included in legal provisions (a point in favor of the objective method); the subjective method can also be translated into law by the much more specific system of quite simply using legislation for establishing a list of debtors, including their respective liabilities.

A general conclusion on the overall suitability of one method or the other cannot be given in a study of this type. In general, the objective method is to be preferred, provided its results are verified in all cases and adjustments are made where needed. However, its advantages disappear when there are many exceptions. In that case, the subjective method is preferable. As in other cases, the option is largely dependent on the pertinent set of circumstances, which varies from country to country.

THEORETICAL DEFINITION AND
PRACTICAL IMPLEMENTATION

Little doubt remains as to how the levy is to be determined when based on the definition of value increase, which constitutes the tax base of the betterment levy. Assuming that the levy base is the value increase that may be attributed to the public works project, this may be found by the difference in land value. Determination may be made by summation of values before and after the construction of the project, prior to the conception of the project and value on the date immediately subsequent to its completion. In this fashion, not only value increases originating in actual benefits are included but also those originating in anticipated benefits, that is, those arising on account of a firm announcement regarding execution of the public works project. It could also be determined by subtraction, by indicating obviously that the tax base is the difference between values on those dates. This approach could be called the orthodox definition.

However, in almost all successful experiences in this field neither of these methods has been used; instead, the procedure of prorating the cost or part of the cost of the public works project among properties benefiting from it has been used. Furthermore, it may be said that legislation that established provisions in accordance with what has been referred to as the orthodox definition have failed; consequently, the final recommendation of this study also opts, as successful legislations have done, for the prorating method.

In some cases, the issue has led to extensive discussions between those defending the practical application of the theoretical definition and those who felt that it is impractical and that the prorating procedure is a very reasonable substitute offering the additional virtue of being operationally feasible. In the authors' opinion, there is little difference, if any, between these two methods. Both lead to identical results; although this may not be obvious at first sight, it will become clear as soon as the procedures to be followed in each case are examined more closely.

According to the theoretical definition, the value of the property would have to be calculated on two fixed dates, and any existing difference would be subject to the application of an also fixed rate that eventually could reach 100 percent. On the other hand, with the prorating method, the cost or part of the cost of the public works project is distributed among the benefited properties, sometimes weighting the prorating elements pertaining to given properties by means of factors that, in some cases, increase and, in others, decrease the tax burden according to the benefit received. If these benefit-weighting factors are calculated properly, the arithmetical result of the prorating method is exactly the same as that of the theoretical definition, since the tax liability-value increase ratio will be constant for all properties.

Stated in other terms, the method followed with the theoretical definition consists of the a priori establishment of a rate applicable to the tax base, while with the prorating method this rate will arise from a comparison of the portion of the financing borne by each landowner with the received benefit. The requirement for an absolute equalization of both procedures is that the rate should be constant.

There are, of course, cases in which the prorating method is applied without measurement of the benefits received. Cases also exist in which the factors have not been examined properly and therefore the levy-benefit ratio is not constant. This may sometimes be acceptable because differences in benefits received are small and do not justify the cost of establishment of factors and/or the use of a more sophisticated method. An example is the case of sewer systems, where all properties benefiting from the system receive potentially equal benefits. However, on occasion, the absence of benefit ratios is attributable to an excessive desire to simplify design, which, as discussed previously, may lead to problems.

This does not mean that assessment of the market value of a property on two specific dates should be considered impossible. If it is possible to make a valuation on a given date, there should be no technical obstacles to valuations made on two different dates. It is even possible to estimate a future value, as is required (and is indeed recommended) when the betterment levy is determined in advance.

The cost of such a method in terms of time and money, however, seems to be difficult to absorb since presently existing technical procedures would require a duplication of a task that by itself is complex and costly. Instead, the formulation of ratios representing the relative benefit received by different properties is enormously simplified by the assessment of the benefits received by selected sample properties and then interpolating these benefits to all other properties.

The procedure of the theoretical definition should not, however, be totally abandoned. If massive assessment techniques become sufficiently developed, their use may become more practical and economical in the future.

INCLUSION OF IMPROVEMENTS
IN THE TAX BASE

One of the aspects on which no consensus exists is that of whether prorating should be solely based on the value of the land, with exclusion of all types of improvements, or whether all improvements should be included. Existing laws are not uniform in this respect; some include improvements and others do not.

From a strictly orthodox point of view, there can be little doubt that improvements should be excluded. The benefits received by a parcel as a result of a public works project are dependent on the functional link existing between the benefit and the project, generally manifested by its physical proximity. This functional link, or physical proximity, is based exclusively on location of the lot since the improvements are exactly the same whether located in a benefit area or not. In other words, the benefits received by a property are derived from its location and this circumstance is entirely dependent on the parcel.

For example, two exactly identical parcels may be located side by side, and both may have exactly the same value and receive the same benefit from a public works project. However, there is one differentiating item: Lot A is totally vacant, while Parcel B has a 10-story building on it. Consequently, the total value of Property B is, say, five times higher than that of A. With the adoption of the criterion of prorating the aggregate betterment levy value among all properties, including improvements, Property B will be subject to a levy that represents five times that of Property A. If it is then assumed that after assessment and notification of the betterment levy, a 10-story building identical to that standing on Property B is erected on Property A, the owners of the latter will have paid one fifth of the amount paid by the owners of the former, although their situations are identical.

This will be the case if the benefit method is strictly followed, which, in principle, governs the entire conceptual framework of the betterment levy. However, for reasons of a cultural nature there seems to be greater acceptance of the principle of ability to pay, and

it would seem that the application of this principle to a betterment
levy system enhances the acceptability of the system while contributing to a redistribution of income. Therefore, for practical reasons
aimed at attaining public acceptance or at including the income distribution goals of authorities in the betterment levy system, the inclusion of improvements is deemed admissible, although, it must be
clear, not within the orthodox application of the system.

However, as this application would violate the basic principles
of the levy as stated and illustrated above, the inclusion of the value
of improvements should only be partial. This can be done in two
ways. One way consists of taking only the land into account, while
adding benefit-weighting factors to land with improvements so that
at the prorating stage they may absorb a portion of the cost. The
second alternative is that of including the entire value of the properties in the prorating, with improvements, but assigning a lesser
weight to improvements on the prorating scale so that they may be
subject to a lower levy.

It should be pointed out, however, that in some urban projects,
exclusion of improvements will result in a proportionately heavier
levy on vacant land and may be useful as a tax policy instrument to
encourage better land use. It should be stressed, however, that
real estate taxes, because they are more common, can perform this
function more efficiently, provided they can be applied forcefully.

LEGAL FRAMEWORK

One of the most important problems to be resolved is the
manner in which the necessary supporting legislation for an effective
system is to be enacted. Since each country has a different constitutional framework, it is obvious that each country will have to solve
this problem in accordance with its own legal system.

The problem originates in the importance that national consti-
tutions assign to the principle of legality, according to which any tax
is null and void unless it has been established by specific legislation. [7]
The principle of legality in most legislations regarding taxation calls
for acts containing provisions that in general terms identify what is
to be taxed and define the taxpayer, the tax base, and the tax rate,
thereby specifying the legal circumstances that will give rise to the
tax liability.

In the case of betterment levies, the most appropriate interpretation of the principle of legality would be to define the tax base
as the existence of (special) differential benefits derived from a public
works project. The tax base would be imposed on the magnitude of
the differential benefits received by each property and the taxpayers

would be the property owners receiving these benefits, while the levy would be determined through ratios between the amount (not exceeding the total cost of the project) that the authorities have decided to recover and the sum of the benefits, not to exceed the limit of 100 percent.

This interpretation of the principle of legality is in the line with standard practices in the field of taxation, with perhaps the possible exception of the method to establish the rate, which is almost always a fixed rate. However, it appears that the 100 percent upper limit of the ratio of total increase in property values to the cost of the public works project eliminates the possibility for arbitrariness on the part of the tax administration and makes the method fully acceptable, although ultimately the constitution of each country is the last authority in this respect.

In existing practice the equivalent to the identification of the taxpayers has been the determination of the benefit area that defines the subjects of the levy in establishing that they are the landowners with properties included in this area. Some laws define the benefit area as a strip parallel to a road, as all properties located at a given distance from an avenue, and so on. However, most of these laws have failed, at least in part, either because arbitrary assessments have been opposed by the affected taxpayers or because the assessment was not significant since the levy was too low to make the system viable for financing purposes.

It is impossible, of course, to provide for all possible situations under a single act of legislation. For example, the act may provide that the benefit area of a thoroughfare is that area located at a given distance from the thoroughfare. The benefit area, however, may fall off sharply in elevation at one point so that part of it is cut off from the rest and has no direct functional link with the thoroughfare and consequently derives no benefit from the project.

The tax base, that is, the benefit received, also has been defined with certain rigidity by many legal provisions. Generally speaking, the practice has been to take the area or frontage of the properties as the basis for assessment, in some cases establishing variable rates aimed at reducing the value progressively with increasing distance from the project. This method very often has impaired seriously the accuracy of the assessment since a large number of situations may arise, some related to distance and some not, where it is quite impossible to make advance provisions under the law.

Problems also have been encountered in defining and quantifying the rate. One way of doing this is to define it as the ratio between the quota to be financed with the betterment levy and the total tax base, a definition that, in the authors' opinion, would be entirely correct but that fails to specify the amount of the quota.

Many legislations define the quota on the basis of a given percentage of the project cost. This method also involves serious problems, as the resulting quota can be either too high or too low. In the first case, the betterment levy will not be utilized efficiently as a finance instrument. In the second case, the quota will be too high and the betterment levy may not be used in the future to finance projects it could have financed if the charge had been more moderate.

The authors consider this method for determination of the four essential benefit-weighting factors that follow the rule generally applied in the tax field satisfactory, with the only justified exception of the tax rate. Leaving the determination of this rate to administrative decision will allow incorporation of the many nuances of differential benefits into the system and avoid the disadvantages of the more customary rigid legal provisions.

IMPLEMENTATION OF A
BETTERMENT LEVY SYSTEM

As observed in the analysis of the experiences in Latin America, the degree of development of betterment levies varies widely from country to country. In some countries, this system is practically nonexistent; in others, betterment levies have reached a limited degree of development over time but their success is disappointing; still other countries, such as Mexico, have an excellent system and some of them, like Colombia, have developed a system of betterment levies that has reached a truly remarkable level of sophistication and efficiency.

From a technical viewpoint, Colombia offers the example with the greatest potential for imitation. This is particularly interesting when it is recognized that the technical sophistication reached in Colombia has allowed for the transformation of betterment levies into an important source of public revenue and has made it possible to utilize fully their potential as a secondary fiscal instrument.

However, it must be remembered that Colombia has reached this level only after decades of experimentation, during which it continuously has been improving the systems through public debate and has confronted numerous setbacks in the execution of betterment-levy-financed public works projects. As a result of that experience, Colombia has built up a pool of local technical staff with long-standing experience in property value assessment methods, having learned how to design projects financed with betterment levies imposed with a minimum amount of objection from taxpayers.

Furthermore, in Colombia, taxpayers, at least in urban areas, have grown used to the fact that there is practically no public infrastructure project that is not financed by the betterment levy. This has been accepted because of a long-standing experience that value increases are normally above costs. For this reason, community opposition to betterment levies has been minimal, although some recent experience has presented some problems.

In summary, the combination of highly developed techniques in the hands of local experts and familiarity of the public with the system in Colombia suggests that the best possible results may be expected; that is, high proportions of public project financing (often as high as 100 percent) are possible through sophisticated procedures developed by local technicians.

The situation is surely different in countries where there is no experience with the betterment levy or where the tax levy has been in use for a long time with only low revenue yields. If these countries (they undoubtedly represent the majority of the experiences reviewed) wish to make efforts to establish a betterment levy system of certain importance, Mexico may serve as the best example. While not reaching Colombia's level of sophistication, it has developed the technique sufficiently to make it an important source of financing. Mexico may well continue to perfect its mechanisms in the future, bringing it up to Colombia's level, as soon as the authorities and taxpayers are ready for a system of this kind. Reaching the level attained by Colombia does not necessarily imply copying the Colombian system, since local problems differ and different solutions may exist that are equally valid. Rather, it implies resolving the problems of each country, area, or city in the manner best suited to its needs, with the necessary refinement and sophistication to raise the yield of the levy to levels sufficient for ensuring a suitable volume of public works construction.

Mexico's system is perhaps less refined than that of Colombia, but it is also less complex. This is partly because it uses fewer benefit-weighting factors and partly because, instead of assigning different rates to each property, it divides the benefit area into subareas and assigns uniform factors to all properties within a given subarea.

There are a number of other conditions that must be observed to ensure a successful implementation of a betterment levy system. One condition is that the application of the system should not be initiated with a large-scale project. This condition minimizes the impact of possible mistakes and allows for quick remedies. Moreover, smaller projects normally generate fewer technical problems and the problems that do arise are easy to solve. This is not, of course, a recommendation that is easy to follow. A country that is seeking to adopt a system of betterment levies usually will be determined to apply it to a specific project, which usually is a large project. Nevertheless, it is a recommendation that should be observed whenever possible.

A second condition is that, precisely because of a lack of experience of the local technical staff, technical procedures should not be too sophisticated. On the other hand, they should also not be too simplistic. Excessively simple procedures sometimes result in the imposition of aribitrary levies, with the result that the revenue yields remain too low to justify the administrative costs of the system. In many cases, the balance between these factors depends on the specific circumstances of the project.

Finally, during the early stages of implementation of the betterment levies it is recommended to recover only a portion of the total cost of the related project in order to reduce the likelihood of organized opposition resulting from possible administrative errors. The success of a betterment levy system, like that of many other fiscal instruments, depends largely on its acceptance by the population, and it is, therefore, necessary to avoid repeated mistakes. When occasional mistakes occur, corrective steps should be taken to ensure that adverse effects, in pecuniary terms, not be too excessive.

The foregoing remarks regarding the introduction of the betterment levy system, on first sight, might appear overly conservative, yet they reflect past experiences and difficulties encountered in various Latin American countries. Excessive enthusiasm should not initially be generated for the betterment levy as a major source of project financing; excessive expectations could become a source of disillusionment, which could be a cause of failure for later projects. An initially modest but successful application of the betterment levy system would help develop more elaborate and comprehensive mechanisms, eventually producing a system capable of mobilizing a larger volume of funds for the financing of large-scale projects.

ASSESSMENT DATE

One aspect that generally is not regarded as important, but that, in the authors' opinion, often determines the success or failure of project financing through a betterment levy, is the date at which the differential beneficiaries are notified of the assessment of their respective pecuniary contributions to the financing of a related project (even though actual payment may take place at a later date). The experiences of the countries studied are not entirely conclusive in this regard since in some cases the amount due is assessed before any work on the project is undertaken, while in others it is assessed long after the project has been completed. However, there is a general tendency to defer the required assessment for various reasons, such as administrative delays or backlogs, political resistance or discontent, and greater ease in making a posteriori assessments when the actual increases in the value of the properties can be more readily established.

In the authors' view, however, late assessment of the betterment levy represents a serious error that may undermine its effective implementation. Specific cases exist, even in countries with a great deal of experience with the betterment levy, where there are grounds for attributing the failure of specific projects to unduly late assessments.

One apparently reasonable explanation in support of the authors' position is that, through an understandable, although not legitimate, psychological process, property owners benefiting from public works consider that the resulting appreciation of their real assets is theirs and cannot be taxed once the project has been completed, and consequently resist the imposition of any betterment levy. Such resistance, when politically organized, may result in failure of the entire financial scheme sustaining the project.

Early assessment is an important prerequisite for the success of the betterment levy scheme since it implicitly (although this also may be done explicitly) stems from the strict quid pro quo approach inherent in the benefit principle of taxation. In other words, the best approach from a policy point of view is to establish clearly, either implicitly or explicitly, that the project will be undertaken and property values will rise if and only if it is financed through a betterment levy. Otherwise, there will be no betterment levy but neither will there be any public works project nor any increase in property values.

In addition to the paramount political problem, late assessment also poses what can at times be an important problem of equity. In fact, if the value increase occurs before assessment and notification of the betterment levy, some properties may be sold. The new owner will then have paid for the value increase but will later find himself liable for the betterment levy, while the seller will have benefited from the value increase without paying any tax.

This problem is sometimes resolved by providing that the betterment levy be assessed in an unspecified amount (since information is lacking for that purpose), which in the future will be benefited by the project. The fact that there is a levy on the property can then be taken into account by public notaries when a transfer of ownership occurs.

These problems are a consequence of late assessment, presenting obstacles that only can be eliminated through early assessment. For example, the sale may be agreed upon before the buyer is notified of the existence of an unquantified levy. The very fact that the amount of the levy has not been determined may not in itself be too important

if the betterment levy is low. But if the levy is used as an effective
means of financing, then the fact that the amount of the levy is un-
known may seriously affect the property market by leading to uncer-
tainty in market prices.

However, early assessment also poses a number of problems,
apart from the need to forecast increases in value. As indicated
elsewhere in this study, this problem can usually be overcome,
particularly if there is an existing experience in this area. In fact,
for some reason or other, the situation may arise that a project at
the planning stage for which financing has been obtained and perhaps
expended is delayed beyond the scheduled completion date. This
situation, which experience shows occurs fairly frequently, suggests that provision should be made for payment in installments, at
low interest rates with monetary adjustment for inflation built in, as
indicated elsewhere, with provision for the installment payment plans
to be extended or postponed if for any reason the project takes longer
than expected. While such a decision might well have negative financial implications, it would help to safeguard the prestige of the
betterment levy as a financing system.

The problem of forecasting future increases in the value of
specific properties usually can be solved without difficulty where
existing experience allows for forecasts based on the results of
similar projects implemented in the past. However, if this experience is lacking, as will be the case if the system of financing is being
introduced for the first time, the obvious solution is to make provisional assessments subject to later adjustments. This solution will,
of course, increase the assessment costs since two studies will be
required instead of one. However, it will greatly contribute to the
accumulation of experience that eventually will make such duplications
unnecessary.

DEADLINES FOR PAYMENT

Apart from the time limits for assessment of the betterment
levy liability, it is necessary to provide for a deadline for payment
as well as for a payment system. A betterment liability can sometimes be very high in relation to a taxpayer's immediate ability to
pay. Although it may be assumed that the value of his property has
increased in an amount at least equal to the corresponding levy, the
beneficiary may not have the necessary liquidity or any reasonable
means of obtaining immediate credit to meet his liability. Therefore,
it may be necessary to provide for time installments to facilitate
payment of the levy (in some countries, the payment period has been
as long as 10 years). In some cases, deferment of payment may even

be indicated, and the usual formula in such cases is to add an interest charge to the betterment levy liability.

NOTES

1. Edwin R. A. Seligman, Essays in Taxation (New York: Kelley, reprinted in 1969), p. 444.

2. Richard A. Musgrave, The Theory of Public Finance (New York: McGraw-Hill, 1959), Ch. 4.

3. For further details on this subject, see Raymond I. Richman, "The Capitalization of Property Taxes and Subsidies," in ed. Harris C. Lowell, Government Spending and Land Values (Madison: University of Wisconsin Press, 1973).

4. José Merino Mañon, La Fiscalidad del suelo y el desarrollo urbano (Toluca: Government of the State of Mexico, 1972).

5. See Centro Interamericano de Estudius Tributarios (CIET), Relación entre los catastros físico, jurídico y fiscal, Doc. 788 of the First Pan-American Meeting on Cadastres, mimeographed (Caracas 1971).

6. Republic of Venezuela, Ministry of Public Works, Office of Transportation, draft bill authorizing the creation of a special levy to finance the Caracas subway, determination of formulas concerning the betterment levy for construction of the Caracas subway, Caracas, 1974.

7. Dino Jarach, "Curso Superior de Derecho Tributario" (Advanced Course in Tax Law), CIMA 1 (Buenos Aires, 1957): 93 ff.

3

One of the most relevant, and costly, parts of this study has been the examination of available experience with the betterment levy, which, to a large extent, is used as the basis for the recommendations given. The essential purpose of the study was to establish a link between betterment levy theory and its practice in a single document and to recommend practical steps for upgrading the levy as a truly operational project-financing instrument. To this end, it was necessary to give at least equal attention to both practical country experience and theoretical knowledge and bibliography in the field of betterment levies, and to trade off the information from the two sources whenever necessary in order to make concrete recommendations.

For practical reasons, it was impossible to analyze the experiences of all countries. Therefore, the study was confined to a sample of 11 countries. Although not exhaustive, the sample was large enough to include the most interesting aspects of existing evidence on betterment taxation and to show that the fiscal practices described could be adopted or appropriately modified to suit each particular project or country and to avoid repetition of past mistakes.

This analysis of the existing evidence is less concerned with a detailed survey of legislation on betterment taxation than with a thorough examination of the aspects that are particularly relevant to understanding the problems usually encountered during the introductory stages of a betterment levy system.

The ideas expressed in both Chapter 2 and Chapter 4 are based on the experiences reviewed, although many guidelines have been modified. However, a full understanding of these ideas requires the reading of this chapter. The countries whose experiences were

analyzed contain such diverse features with so many different kinds
of problems that, for the person who may become involved in policy
considerations regarding the initiation of public works projects,
reading the in-depth discussion contained here will be necessary.

The country experiences illustrated in this chapter will show
that the extent of application and degree of evolution of the betterment
levy vary widely from country to country. Colombia, for example,
is a country where the betterment levy has its most advanced degree
of development with a highly sophisticated structure that may seem
excessive but that evolved from the specific needs of the country.
Mexico, in contrast, has a high degree of development of the system
with less sophistication. Its betterment levy system was highly
developed during the 1930s, and, after a period of inaction, its
development was again promoted about 10 years ago.

In Argentina, the use of the levy goes back more than four
decades, but the excessive rigidity of its legal system, precluding
adequate determination of differential benefits, hampers the development of betterment taxation of a large scale. Brazil has practically
no experience with the betterment levy; nevertheless, this issue
has received considerable attention in academic circles, as demonstrated by the extensive Brazilian bibliography on the subject.
Ecuador, with limited practical experience, has attempted to implement one project with interesting characteristics, but failed because
of taxpayer resistance.

Since the use of the betterment levy is just beginning in
Bolivia and Guatemala, it is too early to assess the evidence in these
countries. Uruguay has made some efforts to incorporate the betterment levy into its fiscal system, but rampant inflation has eroded the
financial importance of this source of project financing, because
payments are made over the long term. In Panama, the betterment
levy was established long ago, but still remains a minor source of
public revenue. However, a trend toward growth of technical know-
how in its operation has increased the fiscal importance of this resource. Venezuela is another country lacking experience in the field
but which has developed a very elaborate betterment assessment
scheme for the financing of a metro system. Finally, the Dominican
Republic has just enacted legislation formally establishing a betterment levy system. The realization of this study was an antecedent
it had in mind in the formulation of pertinent legislation.

ARGENTINA

Argentina's experience with the betterment levy has been more
at the provincial than municipal level and has been almost entirely

confined to the 1930s. The levy has been used almost exclusively to finance urban streets and rural roads. [1] Present use of the levy to any significant degree is at the municipal level where urban paving works are carried out through cost-sharing arrangements and, as an exception, in the province of Mendoza, where the levy is used to recover investments made by the province in irrigation and other projects of minor importance.

Strictly speaking, these applications are not betterment levies and are, in fact, not known as such, but rather as cost-sharing paving projects (pavimentos por consorcio) in the first case and reimbursements in the latter case. The distinction between a betterment levy imposed on property value increments on the assumption that these increments are caused by the project and simple reimbursement of investments made by the public sector is admittedly somewhat subtle. Nevertheless, this theoretical distinction has practical consequences on assessment of the tax liability since, in most cases to date, the prorating of the project cost, or part of it, is made by taxpayers in proportion to benefits received, which is not the case with reimbursement systems.

System Used in the
Province of Mendoza

Mendoza is where the betterment levy, under the form of reimbursement of investment, is used most actively. It provides a classic and almost extreme sample of the usefulness of the betterment levy system for the financing of public works. Mendoza is arid, with practically no rainfall; consequently, land values can be near zero. However, when properly irrigated, it becomes productive land, competitive at the world market level, and its value increases to U. S. $2,000 and above per hectare.

As stated, Mendoza's investment reimbursement system, a simplified form of the betterment levy, has a certain significance. In terms of revenue potential, it represents about 50 percent of the real estate tax revenues, although it should be indicated that the real estate tax is very low in Mendoza. In per capita terms, it is below U. S. $0.10.

Expenditure reimbursement systems are used for three basic sectors. First, they are used to finance the debt service of the IDB loan for the construction of drinking water supply systems in small towns. The part financed by IDB, that is, the part recovered from drinking water system users, represents 50 percent of the cost of the project; however, the part effectively imposed is below this percentage. The exchange rate of the U. S. dollar to the Argentine peso rose very sharply in 1971 and the provincial and national governments assumed a large portion of the difference in pesos. This portion is diminishing with the passing of time and recovery is approaching the official exchange rate of 10 pesos to the dollar. At present, recovery is made at the rate of 7 pesos to the dollar so that the effective contribution represents only 35 percent of project cost.

The reimbursement is made on the basis of surcharges imposed on water connection and consumption rates. Although special consideration is given to the financial/social situation of the taxpayers concerned, collection methods are not very energetic and revenues are low.

The two provincial agencies rendering the service and implementing the large and small irrigation projects—the Directorate of Water Works (Dirección Hidráulica) and the Irrigation Superintendency (Superintendencia de Irrigación)—also have reimbursement systems.

In general, 60 percent of the cost of large-scale projects and 80 percent of smaller projects are recovered over a five-year period. Due to the strong inflationary trend in Argentina and the consequent decline in the purchasing power of currency in which recovery is made, these percentages are in fact smaller since there is an absence of readjustment mechanisms.

Distribution of costs is spread evenly throughout the benefit area; in other words, the quota per hectare is the same for all farms regardless of the benefits received. Thus, marginal areas receiving irrigation at a future time pay the same quota as those that receive full irrigation services at the present time.

Apart from the factual reduction of the percentage of works financed through this system, caused by the reduced purchasing power of the currency in which it is collected after assessment, it often happens that certain cost categories that are usually quite important (such as increment costs or increases in the budget for the public works due to changes in prices or in work specifications) are not transferred to landowners, and the actual percentage recovered is substantially reduced.

Systematic criteria are used for the determination of the benefit area. In irrigation zones, canals are classified into three categories: main canals, branches, and spurs. There are four categories of this kind in Mendoza: primary, secondary, and tertiary canals and spur ditches. The systematic method to determine the benefit area consists of defining it as the area served by the canal and subsidiary canals branching from it. In other words, a project concerning a primary canal is assigned to the area irrigated by that canal and to all secondary and tertiary canals and spur ditches fed by it. The costs of a project on secondary canals are distributed among

landowners whose p.operties are irrigated by that canal, by all
tertiary canals and spur ditches fed by it, and so on.

Another sector implementing a betterment levy system of the
cost-sharing arrangement type is that of rural and urban road works
carried out by the Directorate of Highways (Dirección de Vialidad).
Cost-sharing arrangements are usually set up through the initiative
of the owners themselves—a practice very common in Mendoza
because of a highly developed community conscience there.

There are two types of associations. One type is that organized
at the municipal level, usually to finance the paving of minor urban
streets. The cost of the works is paid exclusively by landowners
whose properties have their frontage on the street and in proportion
to this same frontage. The other system is that of neighborhood
associations organized by the Provincial Roads Direction for rural
roads. Seventy percent of the cost of the road is paid by landowners
through a distribution made on an equitable basis, and in a ratio
with four strips 200, 300, 400, and 600 meters wide on each side of
the road; they pay, respectively, 40, 30, 20, and 10 percent of the
cost of the works.

The fact that paving of secondary urban streets is exclusively
paid by frontage owners and not by owners of adjoining properties
and those beyond seems satisfactory because this type of project
usually concerns side streets. Paving of avenues, or more important
streets, that may be deemed to have a more extended benefit area,
however, are not financed through this system, nor is there any
procedure for recovering even part of the benefits through the levy.

In general, the Mendoza system may be described as simple
and easy to administer. However—in view of the importance of this
problem—it does not seem to differentiate sufficiently according to
the increase in value of each parcel, particularly regarding irrigation
projects that may generate large increases in property values.
Although the low degree of sophistication of the system facilitates its
administration, it also weakens it as a source of financing. In fact,
this system is in the same situation as excessively simple tax systems.
The virtues of simplifications are more than offset by the violations
of horizontal equity, found in all primitive tax systems that impose
heavier burdens on some and lighter on others. This leads to the need
to maintain taxation at low levels in order to avoid serious detrimental effects deriving from this violation of horizontal equity.

For example, the fact that the prorating is made directly on
the total benefit area, without regard to the differences in benefits
received by individual properties within it according to the amount
of water that may be received by each, or to their potential productivity, impairs this system of financing by restricting taxation to a
single level. The level is then either too high for the marginal areas

or insufficient for the more benefited areas. This, in turn, leads to justified opposition on the part of marginal property owners if the tax is imposed at the higher level or to a low financing yield whenever established at the level of benefit of marginal areas.

System Used in the Province of Buenos Aires

The province of Buenos Aires, the largest in both area and population, had implemented a betterment levy system for many years. It was used to finance rural road works, a type of project that is of great importance in the province because of its vast territory and high level of agricultural production. However, in 1969, the betterment levy system was repealed. In the course of its last years of implementation, the revenues derived from it were very low: only about 1 percent of the total collection for real estate tax and insignificant figures of less than one U. S. cent in per capita terms. It was repealed because it did not justify the administrative costs involved. However, actual assessments during those years were much higher than revenues. The low volume in collections may be explained by the fact that these collections were made in long-term installments, with the result that the value of revenues decreased because of decreased purchasing power of the currency caused by inflation.

At present, the province has no type of betterment levy collection; although a system has been approved and its implementation has been completed at the internal investigation level, it is not yet in force. The benefit area in the recently approved system is quite large since it has been established as a 10-kilometer wide belt on each side of the road. The law provides a ceiling of 50 percent of the value increment generated by the project for tax assessment, although, as is customary, the amount of the specific liability is determined in accordance with the cost of the project.

The percentage of project cost to be apportioned to property owners within the benefit area is determined on the basis of the following equation:

$$P = 20 + 0.01666 \ (V - 200)$$

where P is the percentage of project cost to be apportioned and V is the cadastral value per average hectare for the area.

The applicable percentage cannot be below 20 percent, in other words, the equivalent of a 200 peso value per hectare,* since

---

*In this study the authors deliberately have avoided expressing

for this value the second addend is annulled. The maximum percentage cannot exceed 66.67 percent, corresponding to a cadastral value V of 3,000 pesos. In other words, the percentage fluctuates between 20 percent and 66.67 percent applicable to cadastral values between 200 and 3,000 pesos, which implies that, for values per hectare below 200 pesos, the percentage of the project cost to be apportioned will be maintained at 20 percent; for values above 3,000 pesos per hectare, the percentage to be apportioned is frozen at 66.67 percent.

Apportionment of the levy among property owners in the benefit area is made on the basis of perpendicular distance between the geometric center of the property and the axis of the road. The greater the distance, the lesser the liability per hectare. In practice the levy would be apportioned as follows:

1. Thirty percent of the amount to be apportioned is equally assigned to the surface forming two 10-kilometer strips on both sides of the road.
2. The remaining 70 percent is apportioned in a decreasing order in accordance with distance between the axis of the property and the axis of the road. This levy decreases very slowly in a straight line for the first 2.5 kilometers, much more rapidly for the following 5 kilometers, and then again very slowly and always in a straight line for the last 2.5 kilometers. When it nears the boundaries of the zone, it reaches zero, where only the above mentioned 30 percent is paid. Decrease slopes are not preestablished since it is provided that these be determined separately for each case.

Municipal Paving Works Through
Cost-Sharing Arrangements

Another system in fairly widespread use in Argentina is that of paving construction with costs apportioned among property owners fronting on the street in proportion to frontage length in meters. This practice has been abandoned by the municipality of Buenos Aires, and substituted with a surcharge on property tax destined for construction of pavements and sidewalks (in other words, paving is financed by the

---

amounts in national currencies since these would have little meaning for the purpose of comparison between countries. However, in the present case, this type of equation leaves no alternative. An order of magnitude may be given by referring to the fact that the cadastral values on which the system for the province of Buenos Aires is based refer to a period when the exchange rate of the Argentine peso to the dollar may reasonably be estimated as being 14 pesos = U.S. $1.

community in general and not by only those receiving the benefit).
In spite of this, many municipalities, including some located in the
metropolitan area of Buenos Aires, maintain this practice.

Conclusions

Two characteristics of the Argentine betterment levy system,
perhaps one of the oldest in Latin America, seem to have had a
serious limiting effect on it as a source of financing. First, there
are constraints stemming from excessive rigidity of legislation. In
effect, all or practically all regulations concerning taxpayers and
the size of the tax liability have been included in a single legal instrument, instead of providing for a general definition similar to that
given for taxes. Since it is practically impossible to provide for all
types of circumstances, this has resulted in tax assessments that
have been out of line—either excessive or insufficient—with the actual
value increment. In Argentina there seems to be a clear need to
make compatible the interpretation of legal principles with actual
needs.

The second constraint is the absence of adequate differentiation,
as applied by other countries through their factors system, to prorate
the tax in accordance with the increase in value received by each
property. Even within the existing rigid legal framework, it could
have been possible to introduce a greater measure of refinement in
the system, as was demonstrated by the problems encountered in
Mendoza, which has also led to lack of horizontal equity either
through charges that are excessive or too low.

BOLIVIA

Bolivia's experience with the betterment levy is extremely
limited. With the exception of a few projects contemplating the
possibility of utilizing this levy to finance certain projected urban
works, it is limited to a single experience at the municipality of La
Paz—of a certain quantitative significance.

As of 1973, the municipality of La Paz enforces a betterment
levy within its jurisdiction. It is levied on properties affected by
renewal or installation of the main sewer network established in
accordance with the cost of the works and enforced by a quota applied
to each square meter of usable land. This levy, in revenue terms,
represents almost 10 percent of the total collections for property
tax, and less than U.S. $0.1 in per capita terms, although this ratio
was lower in its first year of enforcement (1973).

The basic problem encountered with the La Paz system is its failure to differentiate taxpayers in accordance with the amount of benefits received. In fact, although in the case of sewer systems the location of the property makes no difference with reference to the benefits received since a property served by the system is served no matter where is located, absence of differentiation has been observed in regard to the value of the property since the charge is apportioned on the basis of area in square meters.

As long as the betterment levy is maintained at a low revenue level, this differentiation will not be acutely necessary. However, as soon as the levy plays a more important role and is used for other types of projects, there will be an obvious need to introduce differentiating factors either based on value or on benefits received.

BRAZIL

Brazil's experience with the betterment levy has been very limited, since betterment levies in a narrow sense are practically nonexistent. To a certain extent, it may be considered that the betterment levy in this country is represented by a surcharge on rural property tax, assessed on properties adjoining roads. However, besides the fact that the fiscal charge is legally defined as a tax, it also has the characteristic of being an annual and permanent tax, while the conventional definition of a betterment levy describes it as a one-time charge—arising from the value increment generated— even if collected through installments. Of course, a more subtle analysis could lead to the conclusion that a permanent annual tax has a capitalized actual value, which could very well be equal to a betterment levy. However, such an analysis, although vigorous, would conflict with the generally accepted definition, and for this reason this type of experience does not properly belong within the scope of this study.

Another system found in the Brazilian experience that could be considered closely related to the betterment levy is that called a paving fee (tasa de pavimentación), which is applied by most municipalities. This system is much more similar to a betterment levy than the charge described above because it is not a permanent tax but a one-time tax applicable at the time the works take place. However, the more accepted legislation in the municipal sphere defines it as fee for legal reasons.

This paving fee, which is exclusively used for urban road works, essentially consists of an imaginary longitudinal division of the road works into three equal strips. The central strip is financed by the municipality, while the lateral strips are financed by frontage owners in a ratio with their frontage lengths.

Notwithstanding the fact that this system is provided for under most of the municipal tax codes, at present there is a trend toward channeling the secondary urban construction projects through common law, whereby a contract is signed between the municipality, which pays part of the cost, and the frontage owners, who pay the remainder of the cost.

Despite its limited experience (which even tends to disappear according to what was just stated), Brazil seems to be one of the countries that is most interested in adopting the betterment levy system as a financing instrument. This is suggested by the constitutional existence of the system (Constitution of the Federal Republic of Brazil (particularly Amendment 1, of October 17, 1969, Article 18 (II).) the enactment of several laws that have not been enforced due to difficulties encountered with their implementation, and by the fact that Brazil has the most abundant bibliography of all the examined Latin American countries. [2]

One of the most probable reasons why the system has not materialized in spite of the obvious interest manifested is the disagreement among Brazilian experts about vital elements of its definition. While some support the more orthodox definition of the betterment levy, that the tax base is the difference between the ex-post and ex-ante values of the properties, others, from a more practical standpoint, state that the value increment is an assumption on the basis of which the cost (or part of the cost) of a project must be prorated to determine individual liabilities.

This disagreement is so fundamental that Brazilian legislation has alternately reflected both standpoints. For example, Decree-Law 195 of 1967, currently in force, provides for the first position, while Act 5172, which was repealed by it, provided for the second. In fact, Decree-Law 195 states that the betterment levy finds its tax base in the value appreciation of properties located in areas directly or indirectly benefited by public works projects (Article 1), and then states that collections will be made on the basis of the criterion of benefits derived from the project, calculated by means of cadastral indexes to be determined for the specific areas of influence (Article 3). On the other hand, Act 5172 (Article 82, III (1)) states that the amount to be paid by each property will be determined by means of prorating that part of the cost of the project to be financed by properties located in the benefit area and on the basis of the respective individual value appreciation indicators.

Informed persons consulted by the authors state that, in Brazil, a practical implementation of the betterment levy system would be to prorate the cost of the project or part of the cost of the project on the basis of general assumptions concerning the benefits or value increases received. In other words, that the only actually feasible alternative is that provided for under Act 5172 and that the decree-law in force precludes effective implementation of the system it provides for.

It must be stressed that Decree-Law 195 is "supplementary legislation," which, within the Brazilian constitutional system, means that this is legislation regulating constitutional provisions and is therefore binding on all three levels of government. However, the orthodox alternative is not totally impracticable. In Brazil itself, several concrete proposals have been made to this effect. [3] Nonetheless, this possibility, at least for the present and for the next few years, is beyond the technical and administrative capacities of the country.

COLOMBIA

The Colombian experience* with the betterment levy is enormously rich. It has been highly developed at the municipal level, particularly in the cities of Medellín and Bogotá. It is also well developed at the national level and, to a lesser degree, at the departmental government level.

Global collections for this concept have not been compiled in the country, not even approximately; however, it would not be too risky to estimate an annual collection of approximately U.S. $50 million. This figure would imply approximately U.S. $2.00 per capita on the basis of the country's total population (and not only of the population of the places liable for the levy), which, bearing in mind the quantitatively limited characteristics of this type of financing system, represents a quite significant amount.

The degree to which the betterment levy system (known as contribución por valorización in Colombia at present) has been used and institutionalized in the country may be illustrated by the following incidental facts. In Medellín, for example, there is a municipal agency with a certain degree of autonomy responsible for public works construction in the city of Medellín that derives its funds principally

---

*The authors are particularly grateful to Luis Carlos Hani and Alvaro Restrepo Toro, engineers in Bogotá, for their comments on this description of the system used in Colombia. Their comments have contributed greatly to the accuracy of the description, although the statement does not, of course, make them in any way responsible for any errors it may contain.

from the betterment levy. This agency is called the Departamento de Valorización, a name referring to the increase in property values generated by the agency's activities and not to the construction of public works themselves. In Bogotá, an agency with the same name formally existed, but its name has been changed recently to the clearly more appropriate one of Instituto de Desarrollo Urbano (Urban Development Institute).

Both of these agencies have specialized divisions with long-standing experience in the field, while at the national level their equivalent is the National Betterment Directorate (Dirección Nacional de Valorización) in the Ministry of Public Works, which is expressly responsible for calculation of the levy on the basis of legal provisions. Furthermore, in Colombia, there is an entire specialization (which could be called a profession) in the use of techniques to determine the betterment levy. These specialists hold positions in public administration, operate consulting firms (since many of the problems of these techniques are resolved through reports made by these firms), and act as representatives of benefited taxpayers. As will be seen, these benefited taxpayers have a predominant participation in the system through representatives chosen by a special election system.

From the legal standpoint, the Colombian betterment levy system originated in an act of 1921. However, specific use of the levy began in Bogotá in 1938 and in Medellín in 1948. In this latter city, it has been in continuous use throughout the two and a half decades that have elapsed since then, and the city has financed practically its entire infrastructure through this system, to the point that the current catch phrase is that "Medellín is made of betterment levies" (Medellín está hecha de contribución por valorización). An indication of the importance of this levy in Medellín may be found in the fact that, at present, its revenues are approximately equal to those of property taxes. In Bogotá, although revenues are higher in absolute terms, the ratio of the levy to property tax is lower.

The use of the system in Bogotá had several interruptions, frequently due to public opposition because of improper design. In 1966, the system was once again applied, and this time with complete success since, as of that time, it has represented a permanent source of financing. Simultaneously, the national government also established its betterment levy with success.

Use of the levy has now spread to other large Colombian cities, such as Cali and Barranquilla, and serious efforts are being made to promote its use to finance urban public works in other cities and even small towns. The Valley of the Cauca Corporation (Corporación del Valle del Cauca), a regional development agency, has also used the levy to finance certain projects.

Although the betterment levy finances a fairly wide range of public works, road construction is by far the most common type. Paving and repaving of side streets, and construction of boulevards, thoroughfares, and rural roads are major examples of the type of road construction works financed through this system. There are, however, many examples of other types of projects financed through this system, such as sewer networks (frequently implemented jointly with road construction), drainage systems, bridges, and parks. In addition, the Institute for Settlement and Agrarian Reform (Instituto de Colonización y Reforma Agraria) with headquarters in Bogotá, at present is seriously considering use of the betterment levy system to finance irrigation works.

Procedures

Although there are a number of alternatives, the method used for determination of the betterment levy applicable to each public works project and each taxpayer is the following:

1. The first step is to determine the benefit area of the project. In Medellín, the practice is to determine tentatively the area, called "zona de citación" (notification area), which is usually larger than the benefit or service area. The size of this area is then reduced to arrive to the final benefit area when the benefits received by each property are known. In some cases, the benefit may be zero and these properties are then excluded from the benefit area.

2. Once the benefit or notification area has been determined and in this way taxpayers have been identified, a survey of taxpayers is made that covers, in addition to personal data, socioeconomic information regarding taxpayer characteristics, particularly their income level.

3. The identified taxpayers are called to a meeting to elect representatives. If for any reason representatives are not elected, they will be appointed by public authorities. The function of the representatives is to participate in the preparation of the budget for the project and in a study to determine the distribution of benefits and tax quotas on the basis of expected increases in property values. They also supervise the investment of the funds. The representatives have voice but no vote and consequently cannot halt the implementation of the project. They must, however, be provided with all relevant information regarding the project.

4. The executing agency, together with the property owner representatives, conducts all studies required to determine the levy payable by each owner.

5. The final tax records, on which the name of each owner and amount of levy payable appear, have to be approved, before they become firm assessments, by the duly authorized entities specifically empowered to determine these tax obligations. The owner has the right to various levels of review and appeal.

6. Payment is made either in cash at a discount or in installments to which interest is added. The installment payment periods are determined by the specialized agency with some degree of flexibility. There is no system for adjustment to changes in price levels, with the exception of the period elapsing between determination of the liability and completion of the project.

Techniques for Assessment

The essential characteristic of the techniques used in Colombia to assess betterment levy liabilities is pragmatism. Contrary to the situation existing in many countries, where fixed methods provided by law are applied or where there are regulations regarding the manner in which contributors are identified and their liabilities determined, Colombia has no such limitations. Experts determine levy quotas without limitations other than those established by law: total collections must not exceed the cost of the project, plus certain specified expenses, nor the amount of the benefits received by property owners.

This procedure is the result not only of experience accumulated over the years but also of a deliberate attitude on the part of the experts. Experience has shown that all or practically all projects are different—different in nature, cost, and impact on property values and different in the size and shape of the benefit area.

For this reason, legislators have preferred to provide for procedures while only describing in broad outline the method for determining tax liability. Since this method may seem to provide for a rather vague legal support of the liability, in that it only establishes limitations concerning the cost of the projects and the amount of benefits, it may appear rather imprecise. The system also provides for owner participation through representatives and requires that the final results, in other words, the statement in currency of the size of the liability, be supported by a specific resolution issued by a semipublic body having received express powers to this effect. Moreover, taxpayers may resort to several administrative procedures to object to the amounts of levy imposed on them.

Benefit Area

The most common pragmatic characteristic of the system is
that of selection of the benefit or service area, which is equivalent
to identifying taxpayers. Contrary to legislation in other countries,
where the benefit area is defined in general terms (for example, in
rural road construction, the benefit area is usually defined as a
strip of a certain width that is parallel to the road), in Colombia there
is no legal limitation of a geographic type to define the area, although
such a limitation is implicit in the requirements for defining the
benefit area, namely, that property will receive a differential
benefit.

The flexible Colombian experience highlights the many problems
that can arise in situations where firm rules are laid down. For
example, the previously mentioned and well-known rule of providing
that the benefit area be an area parallel to the street or road can
give rise to a number of problems. The benefit area may be interrupted by a river that has no bridge and can only be forded with
difficulty, if at all. It would then be inappropriate to allocate part of
the cost of the road to the owners of land on the "wrong" side of the
river. A similar situation is an urban street with a benefit area
interrupted by a ravine.

In the case of an important thoroughfare, the benefit area may
be interrupted by another important thoroughfare, and properties close
to the latter receive no benefit from the former. In some instances,
within the assumed benefit area, there may be poor districts receiving such a small value increment as to not justify the administrative
costs involved in collecting a betterment levy, or which must simply
be left aside because of income distribution policy. An important
thoroughfare may resolve traffic problems far beyond the two ends
of the road and, in such a case, the benefit area should probably be
extended longitudinally. [4]

The benefit area is often defined very specifically. For example, in the case of sewer systems, the benefit area is definitely that
including properties served by the system. In other cases, the
boundaries between the benefit and nonbenefit areas may be vague,
and in such cases the boundary is placed more or less arbitrarily
where the benefits cease to be important.

Increase in Aggregate Value

Once the benefit area has been determined, or, as is the case
with the most highly perfected example of Medellín, once the notification area as provisional benefit area has been determined, the

next step is to determine the consistency of the legal limitations. In other words, one must ascertain whether the costs of the project plus the permitted predetermined expenditures are more or less than the benefits received by the area. If the benefits are greater, the apportionment of costs is made on the total. If they are not, the apportionment of costs is imposed only partially.

General experience with urban public works projects indicates that, as a rule and with few exceptions, the benefits exceed the costs, with the practical result that in almost all cases the projects are totally financed with the betterment levy. In rural areas, on the other hand, partial financing of costs is more frequent, partly due to the fact that benefits are not so significant and partly due to government policy since it is more difficult to tax rural communities.

In the quantification of benefits received by the benefit area, the rule is again pragmatism. The most recent procedure consists of utilizing the services of real estate assessors who calculate the increase in value found or forecasted for a number of sample properties throughout the benefit area. The aggregate benefit is estimated on the basis of this sampling, and the sample values are applied to the remaining properties.

It must be emphasized that the selection of the sample is not made at random. Properties are carefully selected to ensure that they are representative. This is a task of approximation in which the aim is to arrive at a global estimate of the extent to which the increase in value of the benefit area is capable of financing the project. An operation of this kind may, of course, often imply an appreciable margin of error. Consequently, it is recommended that the proportion of financing obtained through this procedure be lower than the financing estimated and that, for 100 percent financing to be advisable, the increase in value should amply exceed costs. This is usually the case for urban public works projects.

Determination of the Individual Liability

The next step, possibly the most delicate one, is to determine the amount of the levy to be imposed on each of the property owners, essentially consisting of prorating of the cost of the project.

First, it is emphasized that the property values shown in the cadastre are not used for this prorating. In other words, the fiscal component of the cadastre is only used as an additional reference source. Use is made, though, often with improvements to the same, of the physical and legal components of cadastres.

In the absence of assessed values, the operation calls for the use of plot sizes as the basic magnitude for prorating. However, pure and simple prorating on the basis of property area would not take two essential aspects into consideration. First, plots have different values and sometimes widely different values because of per unit of measurement. It can be assumed that the increase in value they experience is, to some extent, proportional to their original value, increasing in a progressive fashion, although not necessarily in the form of a linear function. The second aspect is that different properties, although equal in value, receive differential benefits from the project in accordance with their functional relationship with the project, usually given by their physical proximity to it.

For these reasons, the area of each parcel is weighted with the use of factors that assign a greater or lesser weight to the plot size magnitude in accordance with the elements having an incidence on their intrinsic value and those determining its functional relationship with the project and, therefore, quantify the benefits received. The area weighted in this manner is conventionally known as virtual area. In algebraic terms, this operation would be expressed as follows:

$$V_i = (F_1 F_2 \cdots F_j \cdots F_n)_i A_i \tag{1}$$

where V_i is the virtual area of property i, F_j represents the different factors, and A_i is the physical area of property i.

Then what is known as the conversion factor is found, which is the budget of the project plus estimated expenses, divided by the sum of all virtual areas. It yields the amount in monetary units pertaining to each virtual area unit. In algebraic terms, this operation is expressed as follows:

$$T = \frac{P}{\sum V_i} \tag{2}$$

where T is the conversion factor, in other words, the number of monetary units assigned to each virtual area unit; and P is the estimated total cost of the project, plus the expenses that may be included.

The levy imposed on each property will then be equal to the conversion factor multiplied by the virtual area of each property. In algebraic terms

$$C_i = T V_i \tag{3}$$

Where C_i is the levy applicable to property i. If this term is substituted for equations (1) and (2), the following is obtained:

$$C_i = \frac{P\ (F_1\ F_2 \cdots F_j \cdots F_n)_i\ A_i}{\sum (F_1\ F_2 \cdots F_j \cdots F_n)_i\ A_i} \tag{4}$$

In other words, the amount of levy applicable to each property is the result of assigning to its weighted area the proportion it should carry of the sum of weighted areas. (As used here, the term "weighted" is synonymous with "virtual.")

Determination of Factors

As may be observed in the procedure described above, the most important elements within the system are those termed "factors," in other words, what symbolically has been designed as F_j. Establishment of these indicators is what received the greatest attention, to the extent that some offices devoted to determination of the amount of the levy are known as "offices for factorization."

Factors are, by definition, numbers used for multiplication. In some past cases, numbers were added. In other words, they were added to obtain a factor, instead of all of them being used as separate factors. However, experience has shown the advisability of always using all factors as multipliers since this procedure permits a clearer picture of the final results of valuation.

Each factor aims to express quantitatively some circumstance concerning the property itself, or its functional connection with the project, reflecting a greater or lesser benefit and consequently a greater or lesser levy. Thus, a given factor aimed at representing a given circumstance will differ for different properties, since if it had the same value for all, it would be irrelevant and would not in any way modify the amount of the tax.

The scale of values adopted differs widely. It is common to use values around unity, so that it is clear that factors in excess of the unit increase the levy and those below it decrease it. It is often found, however, that the bases used for the determination of numerical values differ. The nature of factors used to weight the physical area and change it into a virtual weighted area are extremely varied, and there are no fixed and compulsory rules providing for the use of any given factor, just as there are no limitations to the number and type of factors that may be employed. Although some factors are used more commonly than others, experts in this field have almost total freedom to reject those believed unnecessary and to add new ones according to need. This freedom is, of course, limited by the fact that they then have to face taxpayer representatives or even the taxpayers themselves and by the fact that the semipublic body must approve their accounts, which requires an appropriate basis to support each of the factors and a justification of the criteria used. Naturally, the occasions are not few when experts should ultimately change their points of view.

Factors are always positive, since if even one of them were negative, this would be enough to transform the amount of tax into a taxpayer credit. However, some of them may be zero, implying nullification of the tax liability.

It is obvious that if at some time the decision were made to include subsidy elements in the system for properties damaged through some of the aspects quantified, the multiplier process would be inappropriate, since the fact that one of them was negative would make the final figure negative instead of only allowing for a partial reduction. In this case, the appropriate procedure to follow would be that of adding numbers algebraically to obtain a factor.

In the current Colombian experience, however, the procedure used is that of products totally excluding the use of negative factors. In the case of properties having been damaged and eventually deserving credit, a zero factor is usually utilized to annul the tax liability, and budgetary credits are added, as part of the cost of the project, to meet claims for property "worsenments".

The technique for determination of the value of these factors differs widely, with no general agreement on procedure. Some experts systematize their determination through mathematical functions in order to make results more objective, while others sustain that there are always exceptions to these procedures where it is necessary to modify the results of the mathematical procedure, and therefore they prefer to evaluate indicators by more subjective methods.

Types of Factors

Several of the more generally utilized factors will now be reviewed. It should be kept in mind that none of them can be taken as being applicable to all cases without exception. Some factors are used only rarely. But it may even be said that the list is unlimited since it is possible to add freely new factors for specific cases.

Ideal, or Basic, Factor

The first and most important factor is the one applied for the benefits received by the properties. It concerns measurement of the benefits received by each property in the form of indexes, in other words, not in absolute terms quantified in money but in abstract numbers.

Obviously there is some overlapping between this task and the previous task of determining the global assessment of the value increases received by the benefit area as a whole in order to examine whether those value increases offer the possibility of financing all or only part of the cost of the project. However, these two processes differ in two important respects.

First, the former process consists of measurement in absolute terms. In other words, the emphasis is on investigating the amount of overall value increases received by the benefit area, while in the latter case measurement is made in relative terms; emphasis is on investigating the relative position of each property in regard to benefits received and quantifying it in abstract numbers.

Second, the overall quantification is usually a rough estimate to inform pertinent authorities on the possibility of financing the project through the betterment levy, and a significant margin of error will need to be tolerated. This is acceptable because the final decision involves financing a considerably lesser amount than the total value increase generated by the levy. In the latter case, the measurement must be more careful since it affects the interests of individuals.

This factor is sometimes called the basic factor because it provides the first basis for weighing. In other words, it purely and simply refers to benefits, and is sometimes called the ideal factor because measurements are made in principle assuming that all properties have ideal shapes and measurements. It is defined in a way that allows for later modification by other factors.

In determining the magnitude of the indicator, several elements are taken into consideration. Some are implicit and others are systematically quantified in the form of subindicators. The elements or subindicators to be taken into consideration are basically the following:

Distance between the property and the project: not in a straight line but via existing roads. Obviously, the greater the distance, the smaller the value of this subfactor.

Bottling-in of the property: in other words, the measure in which existing services have isolated the property, since it is also the measure of the increased benefits received by the property through construction of the project—providing the services that were previously restricted are greater.

Current exploitation: reflecting the importance of the area through which the project runs, according to the quality of existing construction, the quality of existing businesses, and so on. The greater the quality, the greater the subfactor, since the benefits received by the properties will also be greater.

Constraints on use: in other words, with the existence of elements negative to the lot, the greater the significance of constraints the lesser the importance of this subfactor. For example, properties close to an airport may be less desirable and are consequently assessed taking aircraft noise into account. Similarly, there may be a railway line cutting the project and, assuming that the land affected has not been previously excluded in determining the benefit area, this circumstance may be accounted for by making this subfactor equal to zero, thereby totally eliminating the levy.

As may be observed, the first two subfactors concretely refer to the relationship between the property and the project, while the last two subfactors are aspects to be normally taken into account in valuation procedures in order to determine adequately the value of a given property without reference to any public works project.

The practical way of determining the ideal or basic factor, currently quantified with reference to value 100 instead of unity, consists of working on the basis of plans of the benefit area. Within this area, a given property is identified in principle as receiving the greatest benefits. This will normally be a parcel with nearly ideal dimensions (in Colombia, a rectangle 10 by 25 meters, or about 30 by 80 feet). A value of 100 is assigned to this lot.

The next step is to identify those properties within the benefit area receiving less benefits. These properties may, for example, receive a value 5. Subsequently, a small number of intermediate properties are identified (normally not more than 20) ensuring that these properties are representative of others surrounding them, and intermediate values are assigned to the same, in other words, values between 5 and 100. At this stage it is not impossible to find certain properties receiving greater benefits than those previously selected as the most benefited or less benefited. In this case, the properties are assigned values above 100 or below 5, down to zero.

Once this process has been completed (normally by highly specialized personnel), it is possible to assign ideal factor indexes to all other properties on the basis of linear interpolation methods that may be assigned to lower level experts. (Attention is drawn to the similarity between this procedure and that used by experts in personnel administration for job evaluation.)

It is again advisable to stress the fact that determination of the ideal factor is made on the basis of the assumption that the properties have ideal shapes and dimensions. This applies because, with respect to the shape of the land, there is another factor (that will be described) that modifies the levy burden according to the form of the property as concerns surface, and this element is taken into account in calculating the size of each property.

Finally, it should be mentioned that this factor is the most commonly used factor in weighting procedures. However, this does not detract from the previous statement that not every factor always appears, since there are cases in which it has not been used. For example, the ideal factor was totally eliminated from the financing of the sewage and drainage network of Bogotá, a very large project with a total cost of approximately U.S. $40 million. This was the case because the benefit is normally the same for all properties served, and consequently there is no purpose in using a factor having the same value in almost all cases.

Regarding sewage systems, it should be noted that all properties served receive exactly the same benefit. The same can be said for drainage systems in most cases, since Bogotá is essentially level. However, there are some exceptions where properties located at a lower level than the remainder of the city are exposed to flooding and consequently receive greater benefits. Likewise, there are properties located at higher levels than the remainder of the city and consequently receive less benefits. A special factor was applied for these cases, called the special benefit factor. This factor is greater than unity for properties located below the level of the remainder of the city and smaller than unity for land located in higher places.

Shape-of-the-Lot Factor

As stated above, the basic factor is established on the basis of lots having an ideal shape. However, whenever the shape is not ideal, obviously both the value of the property and the benefits received will change. In general, it is believed that parcels with greater frontage in relation to their perimeter have a greater value per surface unit and consequently receive a greater value increment because of a public works project. Thus, the factor must be derived from a systematic ratio established between the perimeter and the frontage, meeting the condition that the factor be smaller the larger the perimeter and greater the larger the frontage.

According to research conducted in Colombia, the systematic ratio is the following:

$$I = 3.9174 \, (F - 1)^{0.144} : P^{0.404}$$

where I represents the shape of the lot factor, F represents the frontage (in meters), and P represents the perimeter (in meters).

Socioeconomic Factors

Public works projects often benefit population classes with different socioeconomic characteristics. This aspect is determined through surveys. The Colombian system provides for this aspect in its lower taxation for low-income groups by assigning a factor of 1 to the high-income groups and factors lower than 1 to low-income groups. Thus, the tax liability is modified to the detriment of high-income groups and in favor of low-income groups.

This practice obviously departs from orthodox methods since it takes into consideration ability to pay within a system essentially characterized by the benefit principle. Its use in the Colombian system, however, seems to have greatly facilitated acceptance of the system. It is not only accepted by those favored by it but even by high-income groups, who find it reasonable even though it is against their interests.

Zoning Factor

According to the master plan for the development of Bogotá, the city is subdivided into zones classified as high density (small lots), medium density (medium-sized lots), and low density (large lots). Usually (although there are exceptions) the unit value of land is greater the higher the density, and consequently these cases are subject to application of a weight factor to reflect this relatively higher value.

Since high-density zones, that is, smaller lots, enclose low-income areas, the zoning classification factor to a certain degree offsets the socioeconomic factor. That is why some experts prefer to dispense with both. However, while it is true that the two factors have an opposite trend and tend to offset each other, effective offsetting would depend on the adoption of exactly inverse values. In other words, the offsetting would occur if a district were assigned a socioeconomic factor of 0.80 and the zoning factor 1.25. Nevertheless, decisions concerning these two factors are made independently and consequently the offsetting may only be partial.

This ratio is fully applied in districts that have already been developed. Where there are vacant zones still awaiting development, the factor applicable to the zone is applied with a 30 percent reduction for possible surrender of the land for public roads when development actually takes place. No discount is made for the shadow interest pertaining to the time elapsing between the collection date and the effective development date, so as to encourage property owners to improve their properties.

Change in Potential Land-Use Factor

Often a public works project, particularly if fairly large, may change the use of land, for example, from residential area to commercial or vice versa, making it more or less valuable. In such cases, factors are applied to adjust the levy as a consequence of the possible change.

Topographic Factor

Urban land presenting topographic unevenness has a lesser value since construction on the same involves significantly higher cost per unit of area covered. In the same manner, rural land offering notorious topographic differences is more costly to exploit from an agricultural point of view. In order to take account of this fact, the value is reduced by means of ratios below unity in those cases in which topography thus affects the value of land.

Recently, the value of this factor has been questioned in regard to urban land. It seems that in spite of the higher cost of construction, uneven parcels have a special attraction for high-income brackets, due to the possibilities they offer architects to design more esthetically valuable structures. However, some experts insist on maintaining the topographic factor and correcting this aspect through a surcharge on the socioeconomic factor.

Institutional Factor

As a rule, there are no exemptions in Colombia's betterment levy system. However, there are instances in which reduction, and even total exemption, of the levy is inevitable, as is the case with public welfare institutions, educational establishments, and charitable organizations. In these cases, what is applied is called the institutional factor, which offers levels below 1, thus implying reduction of taxation. It even reaches zero levels, implying total exemption.

Potential Access Factor

The distance from the property to the public works project is always calculated via existing streets and not in a straight line. But the distance may be greater when there is a need to circumvent an undeveloped area to have access to the project. When this area is eventually developed, access to the project will be more direct, which means that there is greater potential benefit. For this reason, a factor greater than unity is applied—as a result of correcting the distance calculated under the basic factor minus a discount for the time that will elapse as of payment of the tax and development of the vacant area—since this only represents a future benefit.

In the analysis of the factor concerning classification into zones, mention was made of the fact that vacant areas were subject to application of the factor with a 30 percent discount for possible transfer of

the land for public roads or highways. But no discount was made
since the value increment was potential, and this was a kind of penalty
applied to owners for reasons of urban development policy. In this
case, the discount is applied since the development of the vacant zone
accounting for the benefit increase is not under the control of the
owner.

Current Use Factor

Elsewhere in this study, mention was made of the possibility of
including structures in the tax base (see Inclusion of Improvements in
the Tax Base in Chapter 2). In Colombia, as a rule, no tax is imposed
on improvements and the tax base is only formed by the value of the
land. Colombian experts have discovered, however, that imposing
some type of charge on land with improvements above that applicable
to vacant land facilitates acceptance of the system. Consequently, a
value ratio above unity is applied according to the number of floors of
a building erected on the land.

This is evidently another unorthodox application of the system,
again resorting to the ability-to-pay-principle instead of to the benefit
principle inherent in the system. However, Colombian experience is
decisive in what concerns the practical advantages derived from this
procedure.

Quality of the Land Factor

This factor, which affects the levy in accordance with the quality
of land, is specially important in agricultural areas, where quality of
land is, to a large extent, decisive for production. However, it has
been found also that quality of land in urban areas has an incidence on
construction possibilities and cost.

Change in Distance from the Business Center Factor

Often a public works project decreases the time required to
reach the business center of town, as, for example, the construction
of a thoroughfare. This is accompanied by an increase in benefited
properties. This factor quantified above unity is the weight factor for
the value increment derived from a change in economic distance.

The product of the basic or ideal factor multiplied by all of the
factors deemed necessary to modify its weight gives what is called
the real factor, changing the physical area into the virtual weighted
area. A careful study of the nature of these factors reveals that some
reflect the functional link between the project and the property, while
others are land value assessment factors inherent in any valuation

system. There is still a third group with a different role, which is
frequently of a socioeconomic nature.

The functional-link factors include subfactors referring to
distance between the property and the project, bottling-up of the
property and zoning factors, change in potential land use, potential
access, and change in distance from the business center. The land
value assessment factors include subfactors concerning current use
and constraints on use, as well as factors concerning shape of the lot,
zoning, topographic features, and quality of the land. The third type
of factor includes socioeconomic, institutional, and current use
categories. (The same classification is used in General Description
of a Standard Assessment Procedure in Chapter 2.)

It is obvious that whenever there is a cadastral system taking
into account the factors concerning intrinsic value of the land (in other
words, the second of the three groups mentioned above) and also
meeting the requirements of a constant ratio of cadastral value to
market value, it is possible to dispense with these factors. That is,
instead of weighting the physical area, one can apply the remaining
factors to cadastral values in order to obtain what could be called the
virtual weighted value. This would be the specific advantage offered
by a duly organized fiscal cadastre in the application of a betterment
levy system.

One item that the Colombian system does not seem to have
resolved satisfactorily is notification date and due date for payment.
Experience includes cases in which the liability is assessed before
initiation of the project; others where it is assessed during the execution of the project; and still others where the liability is determined
after completion of the project. In some cases where the levy has
been assessed after completion of the project, opposition to the levy
has succeeded in preventing collection of the levy. This appears to be
a more or less natural consequence of the fact that if the levy is assessed after completion of the project, the owners implicitly consider
themselves as owning that greater value and consequently assume that
the levy is not legitimately applied.

In other countries, there have also been failures where the
administration has decided to assess the levy on completed projects,
and these cases may possibly be attributed to the same circumstance.
However, the fact that they occurred in Colombia, a country that has
applied the betterment levy for two decades, is much more significant
and provides support for the hypothesis that delayed assessment is
often the cause of failure. (Appendix V.2 of the Spanish-language
edition of this study contains the two case studies on Colombia.)

Conclusions

In summary, the Colombian experience may be useful as a regional model. However, it may be more appropriate to start with a system based on a similar methodology but with a lesser degree of sophistication.

DOMINICAN REPUBLIC

In the Dominican Republic, no levies are imposed on urban or rural property. Nor is there any betterment levy applied at present, although there is a legal precedent for it.[5] Review of this topic was included in a national symposium on tax policy as instrument for development, held in Santo Domingo in June 1974 under the sponsorship of the Ministry of Finance and the Technical Secretariat of the Presidency with the cooperation of the Public Finance Program of the Organization of American States (OAS). During this symposium the application of two types of taxes was recommended: the property tax and the betterment levy. However, attention was drawn to the difficulties presented by the lack of an efficient cadastral system to support implementation and administration of these taxes, particularly with respect to urban areas. At present, a special program concerning rural cadastres is being developed as a subprogram of the Integrated Program for Agricultural and Livestock Development (Programa Integrado de Desarrollo Agropecuario [PIDAGRO]).

Various public authorities of the Dominican Republic have expressed interest in the adoption of a betterment levy system and the Ministry of Finance has requested technical assistance from the IDB for this purpose.

In January 1975, a draft bill was enacted on taxation of incremental land value increases generated through construction of public works projects that has the features of a betterment levy. The provisions contained in this act provide for a levy applicable to 25 percent of value increases. In other words, it is not imposed on 75 percent of the value increase, which limits the potential yield of the levy. Improvements are exempt from the tax, so that is only applicable to land. For the purposes of the betterment levy, the act defines incremental value as the difference found in property values between the onset and completion of the public work projects through use, inter alia, of criteria concerning cost of the project and location of the property with reference to the same.

It should be mentioned that this act was passed at the time the present study was underway and that reference to the study was one reason for its enactment.

ECUADOR

Ecuador's experience with the betterment levy is almost exclusively at the municipal level. However, legislation has been enacted at the provincial level. There is the unique experience of the province of Pichincha, as well as a complete act at the national level offering some very interesting technical features. The act was implemented to finance an important project concerning pavement of a road. However, when property owners were notified of their assessments, these assessments were never collected because of organized public opposition against the system. The origin of this opposition is generally attributed to the fact that notification was made after completion of the project. This surprised many taxpayers who supposed that the externalities generated by the project had already been internalized.

National System

The assessment system at the national level offers, as stated, some very interesting features that merit examination. The system concerns construction, redesign, paving, repaving, and/or improvement of roads; construction, redesign, and/or improvement of railway lines; construction of bridges, dams, and irrigation and drainage canals; construction of sanitation facilities; draining of marshes and swamps; urban and city development; construction of dikes, docks, and ship wharves; construction of harbors and airports; and all other public works that are classified as such by special laws and so designated by the National Office of Valuation and Land Surveys (Oficina Nacional de Avalúos y Catastros [ONAC]).

Notwithstanding the wide range of possibilities covered by legislation, most of the specific provisions undoubtedly refer to the determination of the levy in relation to public road construction. The system offers two possibilities for the determination of the levy: on the basis of differences in property assessments and on the basis of the cost of the public works project. Legal provisions and the bylaws for their implementation assign greater importance to the second method; and in the existing case—that having reached the stage of notification of the levy due—the determination was made on the basis of project cost.

The levy is limited to 50 percent of the increase in value, which is a very concrete limitation as concerns the first method mentioned. However, regarding the second method, it has been expressly established that the lower limit "may not be below the cost of the project," which implies that the increase in value of the benefited properties must be at least twice the cost of the project.

The benefit area is defined for roads and railway lines (in practice, only for roads) as two strips 5 kilometers (approximately 3 miles) wide on each side of the road.

Having established the amount to be allocated from the total cost of the project, as well as having identified the taxpayers through the determination of the benefit area, the next step is to determine the manner in which the total amount is to be apportioned to the taxpayers identified. Two correlative procedures are used to this effect: determination of linear impact and of lateral impact.

The determination of linear impact is made with the purpose of weighting the fertileness of the different types of soil along the sides of a road. In other words, an effort is made to avoid the simplification observed elsewhere to have all properties adjacent to the road pay an equal part of the cost of the project.

For example, assume that there is a road connecting two productive areas across a total desert and that the value of the desert is zero. Then the increase in value generated by the road crossing it probably will be near zero also. However, the productive areas located at the two ends of the road will increase in value. While this is an extreme case, it is clear that the degree to which the value of the property increases will depend on its productivity; thus, the greater the initial value of the land, the greater the increase in value generated by the project. This does not, however, necessarily imply that direct and proportional increases will be generated.

Whenever there is a reliable cadastral assessed valuation that can be used for prorating (on the assumption, as previously explained, that cadastral values maintain an approximately constant proportion to market values), there is no problem because desert areas will be valued at low figures. However, in Ecuador, reliable cadastral values are available for only 8.5 percent of the total area of the country; and consequently, prorating has to be based on property size. There is a need to devise a method to weight the part of the total cost of the project to be allocated to each section of construction, which is not necessarily equal to the actual cost of that section.

In Ecuador, the linear impact is weighted through the same method used by ONAC to assess the value of other real properties, based on a point scale that reflects agricultural, physiographic, climatic, and other productive potential. The law provides that the points applied for the overall classification of the land alongside the the road for 5 kilometers (providing a weighting of the overall quality) be allocated to each of the five pairs of 1-kilometer strips on the basis of the following percentages:

Strip (km.)	Percent	Fractional Terms
0 to 1	33.33	5/15
1 to 2	26.67	4/15
2 to 3	20.00	3/15
3 to 4	13.33	2/15
4 to 5	6.67	1/15

As may be observed, these proportions decrease linearly through an arithmetical process similar to that called the sum of the digits, used for depreciation of a firm's fixed assets. These calculations determine the liability imposed on each hectare of land. From this, the liability for each property is obtained on the basis of hectares.

The liability assigned to each property is then multiplied by factors representing the type of soil of the property, ranging from 1 to 0. In other words, the above-mentioned points are weighted in a way that may either leave them unchanged or reduce them, perhaps even to zero, according to the type of property. A property may range from optimum quality in which case it rates 1, all the way to desert or swamp, clearly deserving a zero rating. Obviously, the fiscus has to pay the differences whenever the factor is below 1.

The law also provides that a levy is due on properties located 6 kilometers or less from towns with 10,000 or more inhabitants, receiving a surcharge ranging from 10 to 100 percent. The surcharge is levied in accordance with the importance of the town, and is higher the closer the property is to the town, on the basis of the following table:

	Distance Between Town and Property Via the Road, in Kilometers					
	1	2	3	4	5	6
	Percent of Surcharge					
Over 500,000 population	100	80	60	40	20	10
300,000 to 500,000	80	60	40	20	10	0
100,000 to 300,000	60	40	20	10	0	0
50,000 to 100,000	40	20	10	0	0	0
25,000 to 50,000	20	10	0	0	0	0
10,000 to 25,000	10	0	0	0	0	0
Under 10,000	0	0	0	0	0	0

As in the previous example, the fiscus had to defray liabilities applicable to properties receiving a factor allocation below 1. In this case, since the factor is always 1 or above, the fiscus receives the difference that may or may not offset the shortfall resulting from the use of the other procedure.

To summarize, and following the procedure as described by Ecuadorian regulations, the assessment process would consist of the following steps:

1. Multiply the number of kilometers of road in each area by the zone score, in other words, by the score in points applicable to the overall quality of land, in order to establish a ratio of points per kilometer for each zone. In algebraic terms, the operation would be as follows:

$$\text{Points/kilometer} = P_i K_i$$

where P_i represents the points reflecting the overall quality of the land in zone i and K_i represents the number of linear kilometers of the road sector within zone i.

2. The total cost of the infrastructure project is divided by the sum of the points per kilometer of all areas determined for the project in order to obtain a ratio of monetary units per points per kilometer. Interpreted in symbolic terms, this operation is as follows:

$$\text{Sucres/points/kilometer} = \frac{C}{\sum K_i P_i}$$

where C represents the total cost of the project.

3. The indicator found through the above procedure is multiplied by the points assigned to each zone to establish the average per linear kilometer for each of the areas affected by the project. In other words,

$$\text{Average levy per kilometer in zone i} = \frac{C P_i}{\sum K_i P_i} \ .$$

4. The average levy per kilometer for each zone is multiplied by the percentage of lateral influence expressed in fractions of unity to obtain the per kilometer liability for each strip in accordance with its location in relation to the road. In other words,

Levy per linear kilometer in zone i, strip j, according to location in
relation to the road $= \dfrac{C\, P_i N_j}{\sum K_i P_i}$

where N_j represents the decreasing levy index based on distance to the
road as a fraction of unity, specifically, 0.3333, 0.2667, 0.1333, or
0.0667 of strip j.

   5. The value thus obtained is divided by the 200 hectares in
each square kilometer of lateral influence on both sides of the road to
obtain the levy per hectare on the basis of linear and lateral influence.
In other words,

Levy per hectare in zone i, strip j $= C\, \dfrac{P_i N_j}{200 \sum K_i P_i}$

   6. The levy per hectare is multiplied by the ratios indicating
individual quality of the land and distance of the property from the
closest town and then by the area to obtain the tax liability for each
property. In other words,

$$t_{mji} = C\, \frac{S_m P_i N_j O_m R_m}{200 \sum K_i P_i}$$

where t_{mji} represents the levy assigned to property m on strip j in
zone i. S_m represents the total area of property m (in hectares). If
a property overlaps two or more zones or two or more strips, S represents each portion of the area included in the strip and uniform zone
to then unify the applicable liabilities. O_m represents the indicator
reflecting individual quality of land for property m. R_m represents
the indicator pertaining to distance between property m and the
closest town, expressed as a fraction of unity plus 1.

Provincial System

   The act governing the provincial level in Ecuador provides for
recovery of 60 percent of the cost of the road from owners of land
adjoining any highways built, distributed as follows: (1) Thirty percent
will be allocated to owners of land located on the 200-meter strips on
both sides of the road. (2) Twenty percent will be apportioned to the
owners of land on strips between 200 and 400 meters on both sides of
the road. (3) Ten percent will be apportioned to owners of land on
strips between 400 and 1,000 meters on both sides of the road. These

percentages are apportioned to owners of the properties specified in accordance with the value of these properties.

In general, this power to levy a betterment charge has not been exercised in Ecuador. The single exception is the province of Pichincha, including the city of Quito, where levies have been used for the construction of a 14-kilometer two-lane highway. Since collections are made over a 10-year period, the revenues collected to date have been very moderate.

Due to the absence of a cadastre, the value of properties has had to be specially appraised by a firm of consultants for application of the betterment levy.

City of Quito

The municipality of Quito makes fairly extensive use of the betterment levy on the basis of the express authorization to this effect provided by the Act Governing Municipalities (Ley del Régimen Municipal, 1971, Articles 415 ff.). Although the act authorizes municipalities to make use of the betterment levy for a variety of projects, generally it has been used for projects involving the pavement of public roads.

The cost of paving is recovered in accordance with the following financing plan:

1. A portion, usually representing 40 percent, is collected from frontage owners pro rata with their respective frontages on the road.
2. A portion, also usually 40 percent, is collected from the same frontage owners pro rata with the respective values of their properties, including both land and buildings.
3. The remaining 20 percent is recovered in the same way as item 2 whenever the project concerns side streets. Whenever projects concern thoroughfares of general interest, this 20 percent is apportioned to the entire city by a surcharge on property taxes.

In the construction of one important thoroughfare, the levy was not only apportioned among frontage owners and the entire city but also among owners of side street properties up to 65 meters from the road, on a pro rata basis with property values.

Conclusions

In summary, with the exception of the municipal level, where a system very similar to that of cost sharing is applied, actual experience in Ecuador is limited. The act at the national level offers some very interesting technical features. However, it would be premature to attempt to evaluate its effectiveness because it has only been applied once and, on that occasion, was not taken to the point of actual collection of the levy.

GUATEMALA

In Guatemala there are two levels of government: the national level and the municipal level. It is only at the municipal level, specifically, the municipality of Guatemala City, that the betterment levy has been utilized since 1973. Legislation to this effect, however, was enacted previously (Municipal Code of the City of Guatemala and Regulations of Betterment Levies of July 30, 1970). The importance of the levy as a tax instrument is limited so far, but it has the potential for rapid growth if plans for its use in Guatemala City are implemented.

At the end of 1973, a decision was made to finance 38 projects through the betterment levy, representing a total of $15.5 million, through a levy providing 70 percent of total cost. A single item, the construction of a beltway or peripheral highway, represents more than two thirds of the total cost. The remaining projects are mostly drainage and sewage systems.

The Municipal Code imposes a ceiling on betterment levy financing of 70 percent of the cost of the project. This restricts its revenue-raising potential since projects may well exist (or could exist in the future) that generate an increase in property values greater than 70 percent and that could, therefore, carry a higher tax burden. Moreover, the fact that almost all of the projects planned up to now have been based on 70 percent financing through the betterment levy, with 60 percent financing in a few cases, suggests that this ceiling is being applied mechanically, while there may well be projects justifying recovery of a lesser percentage. The almost uniform use of this 60 and 70 percent ceiling indicates that taxation is high in some cases, in the sense that it exceeds the value increment generated, or that there are projects that are not completed or not financed through the betterment levy because the increase in value is lower than costs.

The determination of the benefit area is made on the basis of the characteristics of the public works project. With sewage systems, the benefit area is those properties directly served by the system; with road projects, the wide zones alongside and equidistant from the central roads.

The criterion followed for drainage projects is different, as for example, the case of what is called the "10-13-14" main collector.

Here the benefit area was defined as the net area drained by the collector, with exclusion of exempt streets and zones. The area was divided into homogeneous sectors on the basis of average income, which was used as the indicator for the socioeconomic status of the landowner.

The apportionment is made on the basis of the market value of land only through use of the following formula: [6]

$$d_x = \frac{D\ V_x}{A_1\ V_1 + A_2\ V_2 + \ldots + A_n\ V_n}$$

where d_x represents the differential benefit per unit or levy per unit (square meter) for sector x; D is the total differential benefit or total levy (70 percent of total cost); V_x is the market value of land in sector x (quetzales per square meter); A_1, A_2 . . . A_n represents the area within the different sectors (square meter); and V_1, V_2 . . . V_n represents the market value of land in the different sectors (quetzales per square meter).

Obviously this is a very simple system, which consists of subdividing the benefit area into sectors, weighting the unit value of land for each sector, and prorating the portion of project costs applicable to assessed values. The system lacks sophistication, however, in that it fails to differentiate within the benefit area between areas that receive greater or lesser benefits, which leads to excessive levies for some property owners and insufficient levies for others.

In summary, the Guatemalan experience is a positive effort to implement the betterment levy. However, because it has only been applied for a short time, no evaluation of its technical quality is possible at present.

MEXICO

The Mexican tax system has three levels of tax authorities: federal, state, and municipal. Basic legislation provides that some taxes are the exclusive right of the federation, but allows for revenue collection by all levels of some taxes, among which are property taxes. In practice, the property tax is a state tax and the tax levied on capital gains from real estate transactions is a federal tax. Betterment levies occasionally are imposed by all levels of government. The most common examples are urban public works constructed by the states and municipalities, although the latter construct on the basis of agreements or cost-sharing arrangements with property owners.

For the purpose of this part of the analysis, the state surrounding the capital city, the state of Mexico, was selected since
this is the government entity that has made extensive use of the betterment levy and has a very modern and efficient tax administration.

In the state of Mexico, a property tax reform was made in the
early part of 1970, at which time a cadastre was completed that included all urban zones. It assessed properties for tax purposes
through a system based on a model of multiple regression that uses
factors to weight location with relation to value centers of development and cost of urban services, characteristics of structures, and
socioeconomic status of the inhabitants of each street. The unit values
assessed are considered to be very close to market values and are
dynamically updated.

The application of these assessed values to each property is
made on the basis of technical instructions. As a starting point, it
can be assumed that real property is adequately appraised. Property
tax in the state of Mexico has a very high revenue yield, representing
30 percent of ordinary revenues, and amounting to U.S. $200 million
in 1973.

Between 1970 and 1974, betterment levies have been adopted
under the name of Aportaciones para Mejoras (Contributions for
Improvements), and used in the financing of important projects
amounting to more than U.S. $440 million. Of this total, betterment
levies will contribute approximately U.S. $313 million, paid in in-
stallments over a five- to ten-year period. Among the projects financed with this system, special mention should be made of a large
urban development project comprising waterworks and sewage systems and primary and complementary road networks (known as NZT
systems), for a total of U.S. $253 million, and the Toluca-Lerma
and Via Morelo roads, costing U.S. $9 million and U.S. $5 million,
respectively.

The Tax Code of the state of Mexico defines the betterment
levy as a special levy imposed to recover differential benefits accruing
to individuals as a result of a public works project. There is an act
that created the betterment levy system, and there are regulations
governing its implementation. The executive branch issues decrees
for the specific implementation of each project.

In each of the projects financed through this system, the following
procedure is used: (1) publication of the decree-law subjecting the
project to the betterment levy; (2) establishment of the Property
Owners Council (Consejo de Cooperadores); (3) execution of project
appraisal and cost studies, determination of benefit areas, and assessment of the quotas or application of the differential benefit calculations; and (4) notification of decisions and of levies to be imposed.

The establishment of the Property Owners Council involves
selection of owner representatives, appointment of a technical

supervisor, and the formal formation of the Council. The duties of
the Council range from evaluation of studies of the project and imposition of the levy to supervision to ensure that the project is constructed in accordance with specifications. The Council's agreements
are recorded in minutes or documents, which later are published for
the information of taxpayers.

The specific studies for each project are made by the public
agencies responsible for their execution and, on occasion, by consultants hired for this purpose. In general, these studies contain an
evaluation of the budget and costs, the determination of the amount of
levy to be imposed on the beneficiaries, the determination of areas
receiving differential benefits, and the methodology for determining
individual liabilities.

Each taxpayer is provided with the basic data regarding project
budget, benefit area, and tax liability through the remittance of the
documents containing this information. The purpose of these communications is to give the taxpayer the possibility of requesting a
hearing, whenever in disagreement with any of the above, and of
having the time to settle any possible claims within legal deadlines.
After these legal deadlines have expired and account has been taken
of the type of objection mentioned above, individual notices containing
the imposed levy are sent to taxpayers so that, at a second instance,
they may become acquainted with their obligations and make use of
their rights to object to these tax liabilities.

The above analysis shows that taxpayers are selected on a case-
by-case basis. The type of project allows for identification of the
differential benefit areas on the basis of benefits received. In most
cases, the differential benefit area is determined exclusively on the
basis of distance between the property and the road, with the establishment of ranges to classify properties according to the intensity of
use of the road on the basis of their proximity to the same. This
system of making special individual studies has proved its operational
effectiveness and is sufficiently flexible to encompass all of the special
characteristics of an individual project.

In the determination of the tax base, various criteria have been
suggested that differ in relation to the characteristics of the project
and of the benefit area. Thus, the taxable differential benefit may be
consistent with the objective elements for quantification and based on
principles of tax equity. The simplest case among those encountered
is the Carlos B. Zetina main collector project, in which the cost of
the project was prorated among taxpayers on the basis of lot size.
The most complex case observed is that concerning the Toluca-Lerma
traffic corridor. This project involves a much larger area and includes
zones with highly different characteristics, ranging from agricultural
land to high-value residential and industrial areas. Here the differen-

tial benefits were determined through assignment of potential value
to land, calculated on the basis of existing assessed values, on the
basis of the following weight factors:

1. Characteristics of the specific area, including estimates concerning
   proximity to the road and land use.
2. Ability to pay, conditioned by the unit value of land and use of the
   same, as indicator of financial status of the owner.
3. Probability of payment on the basis of a ratio to average socioeconomic status prevailing in the area, tax-consciousness of
   inhabitants in the area, and facilities for tax collection.
4. Tax credits through the exemptions allowed to industrialists in
   the tax treatment assigned to their liabilities, which may be
   partially credited to income taxes under legal provisions governing
   income taxes.

The quantification of factors is resolved through assignment of
coefficients to the different zones within an area for each of these
concepts. The application of these factors is shown in a table prepared for presentation of the quotas for each specific case. It was
observed that in each case—and considering specific circumstances
regarding tax-paying ability in the zone and contributions available
from the federal and state governments—a percentage of the cost of
the project was determined as amount to be distributed, which ranged
from 50 percent for some projects to 100 percent for others.
    A more general criterion was adopted regarding the scope of
project costs, which may comprise almost all direct cost elements
and may include costs per project preparation, execution of studies
for the introduction of the betterment levy, administration of the
project, and collection of the levy. In all cases, the interest due on
the credit used to finance the project is imputed as part of the cost.
    On the other hand, the individual liability is only expressed as
a percentage of the base value, or as an amount applicable to each
square meter within each property. In the case of the Toluca-Lerma
traffic corridor, the individual liability was expressed as a given
amount per square meter of land, with a scale based on differences
existing between the tax bases. The methodology used consisted of
distributing the total levy over the total potential area and then
assigning the portion applicable to each zone within the area. The
amount of levy for each area, multiplied by its total area, ultimately
yields the specific levy liability per square meter of land for each
lot. (For a case study illustrating the Mexican experience, see
Appendix B.)
    Mexico also applies, in the construction of irrigation networks,
a levy system that possesses certain features of the betterment levy,

but that does not have the essential feature of recovering part of the cost of the projects from the agricultural property owners benefiting from it. The authority is established by the Federal Act on Water Works (Ley Federal de Aguas). [7] In principle, the system consists of the obligation of agricultural property owners to pay for the total cost of the project with installment payments over a rather longer term period.

Individual apportionment of levies for this concept is made by a surcharge on the fee collected for irrigation services over several years. Thus, its quantitative correspondence with the betterment levy depends on the manner in which these fees are levied. The usual procedure is for the fees to be levied on the basis of a quota per hectare or volume of water supply, which precludes forecasting whether or not these payments would actually coincide with those of a betterment levy in a sufficiently significant number of cases.

PANAMA

Betterment levies in Panama are known as value appreciation charges (tasas de valorización), and have been used in two areas: the financing of sewage networks and urban development. Of the two systems, the older one is that concerning value appreciations generated through urban development. However, the system concerning sewage and drainage works is the more widely used of the two. Each one is regulated by separate sets of specific legal provisions without any link to the cadastral systems. Administration of the levy is also autonomous and the responsibility of several agencies. In the first case, the responsible agency is the National Water Supply and Sewage Works Institute (Instituto de Aguas y Alcantarillados Nacionales) and in the second, the Value Appreciation Department (Departamento de Valorización). In some cases, tax authorities do not participate in the imposition of the levy or even sometimes in its collection, since this is the responsibility of the agency executing or constructing the project.

The importance of the betterment levy in Panama is small at present, although its use is growing. While in 1968 it represented 1.1 percent of total property tax revenues, in 1972, this ratio reached 6 percent, and revenues represented approximately U.S. $0.40 per capita.

For both systems, the benefit area is determined in accordance with the services directly provided through the public works project. With sewer and drainage systems, determination is based on the zone they actually serve; with urban development projects, on location of adjacent properties or properties near improved roads.

The levy base is usually defined as formed by the physical area of the property; however, more recently, the assessed value of properties has been used. Differential subzones are established within the benefit area on the basis of their proximity to improved roads or location in the block. In the case of some small sewage projects, the prorating base is exclusively that of frontage measured longitudinally. In other cases, different bases are established for the main and subsidiary channels, regardless of whether or not they have been built as a single project. The purpose of this differentiation is to achieve a more objective determination of differential benefits. The amount to be apportioned usually represents 80 percent of the cost of the project, plus costs for administration and financing, with the remaining 20 percent of the project defrayed by the state.

Legislation governing sewage works provides for three types of benefit areas: full-benefit areas, which previously had no sewage system at all; partial-benefit areas of first degree, which had incomplete sewage networks; and partial-benefit areas of second degree, already served by complete sewage systems. This systematic definition is an obvious progress, clearly derived from the benefit principle governing the betterment levy, since it defines the most benefited area and consequently the area where the incidence of the levy will be heavier because it received less services prior to construction of the project.

The regulations governing urban development projects contain an unusual and interesting feature in that they admit the possibility of credits to the affected owners for "worsenments" resulting from a project. [8]

In summary, the Panamanian system, which is usually administered independently from the central government, is of some quantitative importance, and this importance is clearly growing. Should this growth continue, it is very probable that more complex methods than those used at present will have to be devised for determination of the liability. This evolution is already obvious to some degree in the recent trend to base the tax liability on assessed values instead of on lot size or on linear frontage.

URUGUAY

The Republic of Uruguay has two levels of government: national and municipal. The municipalities also have jurisdiction over rural areas. With a single exception, where a betterment levy was collected that really was a property tax since it was of a permanent nature, the betterment levy does not exist at the national level. This type of levy can only be found at the municipal level.

The Uruguayan betterment levy will be examined on the basis of
a case study of the city of Montevideo (the revenue of which represents
more than half of the total municipal revenues of the country) and on
the basis of legislation enacted in 1972. [9] The public works projects
included in this system are the following: paving, repaving, sanitation,
and all projects executed and paid for by the municipality and affecting
property under the jurisdiction of the Department of Montevideo. Later
provisions included sewer construction. Consequently, the system
includes practically all urban infrastructure projects normally executed by municipalities.

Payment is based on an option between payment in cash and
payment in quarterly installments, which, according to the specific
case, range from two to five years. The interest rate applicable to
installments is 12 percent, which is very low if the high rates of inflation in this country in the past few years are taken into account,
including years in which the price level has even doubled. This implies that the real rate of interest has been negative by a considerable
margin.

This negative interest rate or, in other words, the fact that the
growth of price indexes has surpassed the nominal interest rate, has
created a serious problem for this financing system since the purchasing power of sums finally recovered is much less than what had
been programmed. For this reason, it is obvious that the municipality
of Montevideo, in order to make a reliable resource of the betterment
levy, would have to apply a readjustment procedure or to index the
value of the installment payments due.

Problems have not only been encountered because of inflation
but also because (on other grounds justified) the taxpayer liability is
determined at the onset of the project and many special investments
not included in the original plan have to be financed through the general
revenues collected by the municipality. Recently, officials have
attempted to make more detailed plans of the projects to avoid this
problem.

The percentage of projects financed through this system shows
a flexibility in Montevideo that is absent in other countries. This
flexibility greatly facilitates adjustment of the system to individual
cases. In fact, regulations provide that the costs of the projects are
to be paid as follows: (1) up to 50 percent by the owners of frontage
properties; (2) up to 30 percent by the owners of properties located
within the benefit area; and (3) up to 50 percent by a special fund set
up with other resources, that is, by general revenues of the municipality. Thus, regulations permit some flexibility in the determination
of the percentages to be financed.

In practice, large road projects have been financed 40 percent
by frontage owners, 30 percent by nonfrontage owners in the service

area, and 30 percent out of general revenues. In minor road projects, where there is no benefit area with nonfrontage owners, the projects are paid for 50 percent by frontage owners and 50 percent out of general revenues.

In construction of sewers, 50 percent of the cost is collected from properties effectively connected to the system, so that possible later connections and resulting benefits are not taken into consideration. The same occurs with drainage works, where the balance is financed from general revenues.

In road construction, the benefit area consists of the properties with frontage on the road, with the exception of major roads in which case it covers two types of properties: properties with frontage on the road and properties located within a strip parallel to the road of no more than 500 meters that can be subdivided into five strips of 100 meters each, but which normally are only subdivided into two strips of varying widths according to the importance of the project.

This manner of defining the benefit area on the basis of strips parallel to the road project instead of, as is the case in other countries, in terms of physically existing roads generates the problem that some properties may only partly be included within the benefit area. To solve this problem, current regulations provide that the properties located within the benefit area are those having their frontage and larger portions within the area. The interpretation given to this regulation is that the larger the portion of the total area implies more than 50 percent of the total property. In summary, all properties having total frontage or at least 50 percent of their total area included in the benefit area are considered as included within the value increment zone.

In the case of drainage works, the benefit area is the basin drained by the system. For sewage systems, the benefit area comprises the properties connected to the system, but not those that potentially may be connected to it. Thus, when the latter are eventually connected, they receive a benefit that is not offset through any type of betterment levy.

The method for the determination of the levy among owners in the benefit area varies from case to case. In road projects, the charge is apportioned among frontage owners pro rata to the number of meters of frontage. This is a simplistic principle, since it means that the frontage owners pay for the portion of the road on which their properties front. This principle is often found in legislation, and is considered appropriate for secondary roads where it is fairly reasonable to expect that the value increment will be proportional to the frontage of the property on the new pavement. However, it can be inappropriate in cases of important thoroughfares in which the increases in value of the properties adjoining the road can sometimes vary substantially according to the particular point of the road where the property is located. For example, where a boulevard or a similar throughfare connects two business areas via a scarcely populated area, the properties at each end of the road will appreciate more than those in the middle.

Regarding the part to be financed by the nonfrontage owners, first it must be mentioned that a primary apportionment is made between the different adjoining strips in a decreasing percentage as the properties are farther removed from the project. Legislation does not refer to any mathematical law concerning the manner in which the liability decreases as the strips are farther away from the project. But in practice, and for most cases, in which, as stated, only two strips are set up, the 30 percent of the project to be assigned to the nonfrontage owners is apportioned by assigning 20 points to the first strip and 10 to the second. Once this primary apportionment has been made, the levy is imposed for each property owner in accordance with the assessed value of the property, including buildings.

Allocation of costs for drainage and sewer systems is also made in the same manner, that is, in accordance with the assessed values of properties in the benefit area.

Mention must be made of a special feature of the Uruguayan regulations in that frontage property owners are defined separately from those included in the benefit area. In strict terms, frontage owners should also be included in the benefit area. However, from a practical standpoint, the distribution between the frontage benefit area property owners and nonfrontage benefit area property owners in the Uruguayan case is due to the different prorating criteria used for these two cases.

Elsewhere in this study it has been said that it is debatable whether or not improvements or structures are to be included in the levy, although to a point this should facilitate collections. However, apart from this overall aspect, and admitting the existence of an appropriate cadastre, some comments should be made on the Uruguayan system.

The criterion is considered appropriate for sewer systems in which, leaving aside failure to include potential connections to the system, it seems reasonable to apportion its cost among the properties served pro rata to assessed values. In the case of road projects, however, and as already pointed out for frontage owners, properties with the same assessed value located in different parts of the road may be subject to different value increases. On the other hand, in the case of drainage works, it is obvious that properties located in the lower parts of the drainage basin will receive greater benefits than those located near its edge.

The yield of the betterment levy in the Montevideo municipality represents approximately 1 percent of total land tax revenues, and in per capita terms, slightly over U.S. $0.10.

It is clear that the Uruguayan system requires greater technical sophistication if it is to become a significant source of revenue, as well as a monetary correction feature—at least while the inflationary trend continues and installment payments continue to be liberally applied.

VENEZUELA

Although Venezuela has enacted and has in effect two acts dealing with the betterment levy[10] that are based on individual assessment to determine the respective value increases generated, in practice the system has not been applied to any specific project. The only experience having something in common with the betterment levy, and that could to a certain extent be assimilated by it, is the fact that many properties are expropriated for the construction of public works, particularly roads, and their owners do not receive any compensation for the expropriation, on the assumption that the road construction enhances the value of their remaining property.

This criterion, which in a way could be considered as a betterment levy collected in kind, seems appropriate in those cases where properties are very large—in other words, in instances where expropriation of a strip of land leaves sufficient land untouched as to allow for an increase equal or greater than the value of the land expropriated. However, this levy "in kind" is arbitrary in that it neglects to take into consideration the existence of property owners benefited by a public works project who are not subject to any kind of expropriation. The violation of horizontal equity is quite clear in this case.

The city of Caracas has formulated a project for construction (already underway as this is written) of a subway system designed to cross the city, which has a longitudinal shape. Part of the financing of this project is to be obtained through a betterment levy system. In this case, a specific project has been drafted by an ad hoc committee on the entire procedure for apportionment of the levy, and the draft project includes a draft bill.[11]

The system is designed on the basis of determination of the portion of project costs to be financed through betterment levies apportioned to all benefited landowners. In other words, there is no individual assessment of the value increment received by each property, although an estimate is made to the effect that the aggregate selected is not to exceed the value increment received by all of the properties involved.

In this case, the aggregate is formed by the part of the project costs to be defrayed by the municipality on the basis of agreements signed with the national government, and representing 50 percent of the cost of the subway infrastructure. In turn, this sum is subdivided into two subtotals: 20 percent assigned to the generic area and 80 percent to the specific area. The "generic area" is that receiving overall benefits from the subway construction through reduction of traffic and environmental pollution services.

Consequently, the generic area defraying 20 percent of the cost is formed by the entire city, and the assessment of the levy applicable to each property is based on the following equation:

$$C_{gi} = \frac{C_g I_i}{\sum_i I_i}$$

where C_{gi} is the betterment quota applicable to property i; C_g is the subtotal to be apportioned to all properties within the generic area, in other words, 20 percent of the aggregate cost; and I_i is the amount of property tax paid by property i.

In simpler terms, 20 percent of the aggregate, that is, 10 percent of the cost of the project, is distributed among all properties in the city in a ratio with the property tax paid by each.

This part of the apportionment obviously tries to reflect the aggregate increase in value of all properties in the city resulting from reduction of environmental pollution and traffic congestion. Although this part of the levy is quite similar to a charge based on the benefit principle, it is to be recalled that there is a fundamental difference in the fact that while a tax is permanent, this levy is a one-time charge, which lends validity to the sound fiscal criterion applied by the designers of the project in assigning part of the cost of construction to the entire city.

In the apportionment of the subtotal applicable to the specific area, in other words, 80 percent of the aggregate or 40 percent of the cost of the project, more sophisticated criteria have been adopted, as is to be expected in this type of situation. First, the benefit area is defined as that containing properties within a 10-minute walk from a subway station. It is to be noted that this does not concern geographic distance in a straight line, but distance through existing streets from the door of the respective building to the closest station. In a map not reflecting physical distance but rather walking distance expressed in minutes via existing streets, the benefited areas would consist of circles within a 10-minute radius centered at each of the stations.

In determining the subtotals pertaining to the specific area, the following equation is used:

$$C_{ei} = \frac{C_e V_i K_i}{\sum_i V_i K_i}$$

where C_{ei} represents the specific charge applicable to each property apart from C_{gi}; C_e is the subtotal apportioned to the specific area, that is, 80 percent of the total to be financed through the betterment levy or 40 percent of the cost of the project; V_i is the value of each property, including the value of land, and of existing structures and businesses conducted on the premises; and K_i is a parameter that is a function of the walking distance from the property entrance to the subway station.

In other words, the subtotals applicable to the specific area are distributed in a ratio with land value, values of improvements, and business value, with the amount of the charge weighted on the basis of a parameter, K_i, which is a function of the walking distance in minutes between the entrance to the subway and the entrance to the building, designated as X_i.

In order to define the nature of this functional relationship (which naturally must be an inverse ratio) and to simplify subsequent practical calculations, the circle with a radius of 10 minutes is divided into a circle with a radius of 2 minutes and into four rings with a radius of 2 minutes each from the zones, assigning values for X_i equal to the mean distance within that zone from the subway; thus, there are only five figures for X_i: 1, 3, 5, 7 and 9.

Several types of calculations are made to find the nature of the function relating K_i and X_i. First, that of the inverse function, that is,

$$K_i = 1/X_i$$

Although this type of ratio seems to be the more logical, its results in practice yield an excessive charge for the first area, then abruptly decrease for the second, and very slowly decrease for subsequent areas. This was to be expected in view of the hyperbolic characteristics of this function.

The authors made several tests and finally found an equation meeting the requirement of not excessively charging the first area, decreasing the charge at a reasonable rate for remaining areas, and finally giving a parameter equal to zero to be applied to properties not within the area—that is, when X_i is equal to 11. The following equation resulted:

$$K_i = \frac{1}{X_i^2 + 51} + \frac{11\,X_i - 207}{14.792}$$

This equation gives the following values for K_i:

$X_1 = 1; K_1 = 0.39$

$X_2 = 3; K_2 = 0.32$

$X_3 = 5; K_3 = 0.19$

$X_4 = 7; K_4 = 0.08$

$X_5 = 9; K_5 = 0.02$

As may be observed in the results, the authors of this study have obtained a mathematical equation complying with the objectives formulated. In other words, they have obtained parameters not establishing an excessive charge on the first zone, decreasing in the measure that the property is farther removed from the entrance of the subway at a reasonable rate, and one providing a result equal to zero for hypothetical $X_6 = 11$. This can easily be tested if this latter figure is introduced into the final equation.

NOTES

1. For a detailed analysis of the Argentine experience, see Jorge Macón, Financiación Pública por Contribución de Mejoras (Buenos Aires: Consejo Federal de Inversiones, 1971), pp. 11 ff.
2. A complete Brazilian bibliography on this subject would be too extensive. However, the more important works are as follows: Geraldo Ataliba, Contribuição de Melhoria e Instrumentos Afins para Financiamento de Obras Rodoviárias (Rio de Janeiro: IPR, 1969); Daltro Barbosa Leite, Contribuição de Melhoria Estradas de Rodagem e Valor da Terra (Rio de Janeiro, 1972); Symposium on the Betterment Tax, Final Report (Rio de Janeiro: Instituto Brasileiro de Administração Municipal, 1967); Revista de Administração Municipal (Rio de Janeiro), January/February 1968; Aplicação da Contribuição de Melhoria a Obras Rodoviárias Federais (Rio de Janeiro: Instituto Brasileiro de Administracao Municipal, 1971); Joao Luiz de Moraes Barreto, "Teoría e Prática da Contribuição de Melhoria," Revista de Administração Municipal (Rio de Janeiro), May/June 1969.

3. Barreto, op. cit.

4. For these and other problems of this kind, see Instituto para el Desarrollo de Antioquia, Manual de Valorización (Medellín: Departamento Nacional de Planeación de Colombia, 1974) and Alvaro Restrepo Toro, "Determinación del Monto Distribuíble y la Zona de Influencia en Obras de Valorización," mimeographed (Medellín, June 1974).

5. Ley 1849 del 27 de noviembre de 1948 (Act 1849 of November 27, 1948).

6. Danilo Cruz Morales, "Financiamiento de Obras de Desarrollo Municipal por el Sistema de Contribución de Mejoras" (Financing of Municipal Development Projects Through the Betterment Levy System) (dissertation, University of San Carlos, Guatemala City, 1973), p. 80.

7. Diario Oficial de la Federación (Official Gazette of the Federation) (Mexico City), January 11, 1972.

8. Reglamento del 4 de octubre de 1973, Artículo 23 (Regulation of October 4, 1973, Article 23).

9. Municipality of Montevideo, Decree 15.706 of 1972, Presupuesto General de Sueldos, Gastos y Recursos de la Intendencia Municipal de Montevideo para 1972-77 (General Budget for Wages, Expenditures and Resources of the Municipality of Montevideo for 1972-77), Article 226, Diario Oficial de la Federación (Official Gazette of the Federation), August 11, 1972, pp. 329-36.

10. Ley de Expropiación por Causa de Utilidad Pública y Social (Act Concerning Expropriation for Works of Public and Social Interest), November 6, 1947; Ley de Utilización de Obras Públicas Nacionales (Act on Utilization of Public Works Projects), January 20, 1954.

11. Republic of Venezuela, Ministry of Public Works, Ministerial Office of Transportation, Proyecto de Ley que Autoriza la Creación de una Contribución Especial para el Financiamiento del Metro de Caracas (Draft Bill Authorizing Establishment of a Special Levy for the Financing of the Caracas Subway), Caracas, 1974.

4

CONCLUSIONS
AND RECOMMENDATIONS

NORMATIVE MODEL

The implementation of a normative model for a betterment levy system must be adapted to the various legislative and constitutional requirements of each country. However, any legislation aimed at the creation of a betterment levy system should incorporate some basic features to ensure its operational feasibility, quite apart from the legal formalities adopted.

It is essential to distinguish the betterment levy from other apparently comparable fiscal tools, such as taxes and fees. A doctrinal, as well as an empirical, discussion of these distinctions, based on the tax legislation of several countries, is presented in Chapters 2 and 3. It is appropriate to repeat here that the betterment levy must be firmly embodied in tax codes in order to establish its fiscal character and facilitate the issuance of adequate regulations. This is particularly important since, for operational convenience, the responsibilities concerning administration and collection of betterment levies are often delegated to the agencies directly charged with the execution of the public works projects. Relevant examples are Panama's Water Supply and Sewerage Institute (Instituto Nacional de Aguas y Alcantarillados de Panamá) for water projects and Mexico's Water Supply Board (Junta de Aguas) for irrigation projects.

The conceptual characteristics to be incorporated into legal provisions on betterment levies refer to the following essential issues: the execution of the public works projects implemented by the betterment levy; criteria to determine the magnitude of differential benefits, usually in the form of increases in the value of land and/or real estate in a well-defined area; the instrumentality of a betterment levy as a source of project financing; and the compulsory character of the levy for all benefited property owners.

In addition, legal provisions on betterment levies must regulate aspects concerning taxpayers, coverage, tax base, rate of levy, exemptions, and procedures for assessment and collection of the levy— all of which are prerequisites for efficient implementation and administration of the betterment levy.

Nature and Scope of Legal Provisions

In view of the casuistical nature of the betterment levy, its operational and administrative requirements may well differ from one project to another, and cannot be spelled out in detail in a comprehensive legal document. In fact, the highly technical character of such requirements has represented a serious obstacle in countries that have failed to make use of the betterment levy system despite the long-standing existence of authorizing legislation.

Yet a general legal order must exist to govern the application of the betterment levy and to safeguard the legal interests of property owners. It is within this general legal order that expedient regulations concerning each specific case can be issued from a position of effective legal authority.

It is common practice in Latin America for the betterment levy to be instituted as a by-product of national planning directives, public works decrees (as in Mexico), or organic statutes of project-executing agencies empowered to impose these levies (Panama's Water and Sewerage Institute). This situation hampers collections because, for example, it excludes the use of levy collections based on expedient and lower cost enforcement systems. It also leads to underutilization of the data stored in fiscal records and to distortions in assessment of tax liabilities within the framework of overall fiscal policy. Therefore, in order to decentralize the collection process, it is preferable to affirm the strictly fiscal nature of the betterment levy through tax legislation, separately providing for the administrative responsibilities that may be delegated to nonfiscal agencies more closely associated with project execution.

Although any set of legal provisions governing a national betterment levy system must satisfy the general constitutional and legislative framework of the country, it appears advisable to incorporate such provisions into three legal instruments:

1. The tax code, formally instituting the betterment levy as a component of the tax system, and defining its conceptual characteristics.

TABLE 4.1

Betterment Levy Normative Model: Scope and Characteristics of Legal Provisions

Instrument Provisions	Tax Code	Legislation on Betterment Levies	Administrative Directives or Decree Governing Financing of Public Works Through the Betterment Levy
	Conceptual definition of special levies and the betterment levy.	General provisions governing the substantive and objective aspects of the levy: Objectives Taxpayers Levy base Individual liabilities Exemptions Procedure for issuance of specific regulations Billing and collection procedures	Specific criteria for enforcement of a betterment levy, particularly: Description of the public works project Benefit area Aggregate levy Parameters to determine differential benefits received by each owner Individual tax liabilities Deadlines for payment Administrative authorities

2. Betterment levy legislation providing for the substantive and procedural aspects governing its scope of enforcement; the types of public projects eligible for partial or complete betterment levy financing; the determination of tax bases and rates for betterment taxation; and, finally, the procedures for its implementation.
3. Executive decrees regulating the imposition of the betterment levy in each specific instance and, in particular, the areas subject to the levy, the amount of assessments, deadlines for payment, exemptions, and so on.

Whenever the national legal system requires the passing of a specific act of legislation for each proposed betterment levy, a feasible alternative is to include the general conceptual guidelines in the tax code, with specific rules for its implementation under special acts applicable to each situation.

Objectives of the Betterment Levy

In most legislations examined, the purpose of the levy is to recover through the levy all or part of the differential benefits to properties located in a specific area that have been generated as a consequence of the construction of public works projects. From this definition it follows that the tax base is the increase in property value, and the event giving rise to the imposition of the levy is the execution of a public works project. However, it is useful to analyze further the criteria used in defining the tax base and the events giving rise to the imposition of the levy.

Subject of Levy

Although differential benefits can be defined broadly as the increases in value of real estate and/or land, the precise measurement of such benefits poses difficult operational problems. The problems involved in the determination of property value increases are both conceptual and technical. Assessed values of real estate and land properties, generally used for value increase assessment, normally reflect the values prior to the public works project, and the assessment of property values is not always based on efficient or objective criteria. It is generally agreed that "assessed values, although expressed in money terms, only are index values since they are not aimed at providing an estimate of absolute property values but rather of relative values—i.e., the value of a given property in relation to all others—as a basis for an equitable distribution of the tax burden."[1]

TABLE 4.2

Betterment Levy Normative Model: Objectives of the Levy

Provisions	Legislation on Betterment Levies	Administrative Directives or Decree Governing Financing of Public Works Through the Betterment Levy
Scope	Broad concept, expressed in generic terms.	Concepts determined by the specific characteristics of each case.
Definitions		
Tax base	Differential benefits received by real property in a given area.	Specification of the differential benefits generated by the project in terms of increased values, provision of services, connections and communications, and so on. Determination of the beneficiaries, distinguishing between land and land with improvements and demarcation of the benefit area.
Event of causation of liability	Execution of a public works project for common use.	Description of the public works project.

TABLE 4.3

Betterment Levy Normative Model: Subject of Levy

Instrument Provisions	Legislation on Betterment Levies	Administrative Directives or Decree Governing Financing of Public Works Through the Betterment Levy
Definitions	Explicit concept of differential benefit. Statement of the factors that can, as appropriate in each specific case, be taken into account, separately or jointly, to determine the tax base (differential benefit) such as location, land use, potential benefits, ability to pay, present value, area, and so on.	Explicit statement of the formula used to determine the tax base in the specific case and establishment of the weights to be applied for purposes of apportionment of liabilities. Explicit statement of the formula used. Establishment of the weight to be applied for apportionment of liabilities (area or value).

89

These problems have discouraged tax authorities from attempting to determine betterment levy quotas according to actual increases in property values. Instead, the determination of betterment levies for the financing of public works projects is derived from proxies (benefit-weighting factors) of differential benefits, such as physical proximity of the beneficiaries to the project, property size, and assessed values.

Explicit reference to the terms "property value appreciation" and "increased values" under any betterment legislation must be complemented with operations indicators to avoid controversy in their interpretation. The concept "differential benefits" is, for practical purposes, more suitable to betterment taxation than is "property value appreciation."

Betterment legislation must also identify the components of the tax base. Some betterment levies are collected on either land or real estate, whereas others combine both elements. A good case can be made for either approach. On the one hand, it may be assumed that public works projects appreciate land alone, so that the fiscal incidence of levies imposed on both real estate and land would not be neutral. On the other hand, it can be argued that differential benefits cause an increase in value of both land and improvements. A more appropriate criterion would be to differentiate the betterment levy according to the nature of a specific project, the type of benefit received, and the location of the property.

While the exemption of structures from the betterment levy is in line with a strict application of the benefit principle, such improvements are indicative of property owners' comparative ability to pay and financial status, particularly in the case of urban properties.

Since substantive betterment provisions are of general application, it is advisable to give them sufficient flexibility so that the type of real estate holdings subject to betterment levies can be specified on a case-by-case basis through executive decrees or other regulatory devices. General rules should also be sufficiently flexible to identify all the project characteristics that may have a significant bearing on the magnitude and area of benefits received.

Event of Causation of Increase in Value

While betterments giving rise to the collection of levies are inherent in the public character of any public works project, some laws restrict the use of such levies to specific categories of projects, particularly to urban development projects. This restrictive specification of projects seems to be based on the criterion of an unobjectionable identification of those projects that may generate differential benefits. However, this goal is not always attained because differential benefits are determined more by circumstance than by type of project. For example, the opening of a thoroughfare may or may not generate benefits for adjoining properties; if it is an express-way and the area is a business district, it may lead to value decreases rather than to benefits.

Consequently, it seems desirable for the adoption of general rules not to define restrictively the types of projects but to unequiv-ocably state that the betterment levy may only be enforced whenever the public works project generates differential benefits that can be objectively assessed, and leave the specific definition of the projects that may be financed through the betterment levy to such dynamic factors as government initiatives and its financial policies and the preferences of the citizens who may be affected by the levy.

Persons Liable for the Betterment Levy

Two conditions determine a person's liability for the betterment levy: ownership of real property and location of that property within the benefit area of the public works project. The existence of "pre-carious" forms of ownership, common in the Latin American countries, suggests that the concept of ownership should be stretched to include all those having some form of property rights over the benefiting properties. Such is the case of prominent buyers, persons having users' rights over property, real estate holders, "ejidatarios," and persons entitled to relative or conditioned ownership.

The configuration of the benefit area depends on the particular features of the zone and of the projects themselves. The size of the area is sometimes affected by geographic obstacles or political limitations, which may distort the apportionment of differential bene-fits, particularly in urban centers that extend over several neighboring municipalities or states. In other cases, the benefit area radius may be enlarged by supplementary public works.

Sometimes the benefit area is defined on a conditional basis. That is, it can be reduced or enlarged if, within a specified period, any change takes place in the circumstances prevailing at the time the levy was imposed, particularly changes in land use. This is the case, for example, of very steep and unproductive land, the value of which would only relatively increase through the construction of a public works project if land use were maintained, but which would substantially increase if the area were destined for residential or industrial use.

The solution to this problem is to enact general rules with sufficient scope and flexibility to encompass the greatest possible number of different situations. Regarding the first characteristic,

TABLE 4.4

Betterment Levy Normative Model: Taxpayers

Instrument	Legislation on Betterment Levies	Administrative Directives or Decree Governing Financing of Public Works Through the Betterment Levy
Provisions		
Definitions	Broad concepts, including all forms of ownership or tenure.	Location of the owners, holders, or occupants of the specific area defined for each project. In the event of foreseeable changes in land use, regulation of the possibility of change or expansion of the areas originally determined and measures applicable to such changes.
	Broad definition of the benefit area and authority to apply the levy on a case-by-case basis under provisions applicable to each project, based on specific studies.	
	Encumbrance of the property to serve as collateral for the tax liability.	

they should refer to the different types of property defined by the national legislation or to the broad definition of who are property owners or holders, possessors, or tenants. Regarding the delimitation of zones, very general rules should be established and the specific regulations should define the area for each project in accordance with its specific characteristics. They should also provide for cases in which it is necessary to make a qualitative or quantitative change in the zones forming part of the benefit area.

Apart from the owners' liability, the property itself must constitute tangible security for payment of the levy, in the same way as with property taxes. This link between the property and the tax obligation is particularly important in the case of the betterment levy since, given the temporary nature of the levy, if ownership of the property changes hands after the project has been completed, but before the betterment levy has been fully paid, the original owner may disappear and a levy limited to personal liability may prove impossible to collect. In some countries, this is done through legislative provisions, while in others it is necessary to include mention of the levy imposed on the property in the public register, legal cadastre, or land records.

Betterment Levy Base

To be consistent with a strict application of the benefit principle, the levy should be imposed on the increase in property values generated by the execution of a public works project. This, however, is based on the assumption that such value increases can be determined as the difference between property values before and after completion of the project. This method is of little use because it poses complex technical difficulties in finding two distinct valuations, the latter being subject to highly subjective assessment.

An alternative method often used to determine property value increases is to assign each property a value increment proportional to the total cost of the project, prorated on the basis of various objective weighting factors. The procedure is formally sound, since it yields a quantitative estimate of differential benefits. Another method is to determine a tax-base value on the basis of various measurable weighting factors of the magnitude of the benefits conferred to each property. Such factors, among others, normally refer to property location, land use, and current cadastral assessments. The administrative simplicity of this method considerably facilitates the application of a betterment levy.

Both systems apportion relative levy burdens according to some average of benefit-weighting factors, which determine the base, while absolute levy quotas are established through the rate. Differences between them are established through alternative quantitative or conceptual definitions, such as those focusing on current assessed values or on imputed differential benefits. The adequate selection of benefit factors and of the weights assigned to them in setting the tax base is critically important for the success of the system. It is therefore recommended that the selection of the differential benefit factors be provided for under general betterment legislation, leaving the determination of their relative weights to regulatory decrees applicable to specific cases.

In addition to describing the general benefit factors applicable to each case, regulatory decrees should also specify the formula and weights to be used. The most frequently used factors, either separately or jointly, include

Location of the property: weighted to reflect linear or radial distance from the project.
Potential benefits: weighted to reflect the direct services that the project generates for the property.
Land use: weighted to reflect land productivity.
Social aspects: weighted to reflect the average socioeconomic level of property owners in the benefit area, the impact of the betterment levy on their total tax burden (particularly as concerns real estate taxes), the level of tax education prevailing in the area, ease of collection, and so on.
Size of the property.
Present value: assessed value or market values specifically determined.

Quotas

Determination of the Amount to Be Allocated

By definition, the proceeds of betterment levies should never exceed the costs of the public works projects they are to finance. (Benefits should exceed costs.) This condition that the levy should not exceed costs should be provided for explicitly under betterment legislation. Moreover, it is necessary to define what categories of project costs are eligible for betterment financing and what proportions thereof can be apportioned to property owners.

Some laws only consider the total direct items concerning contractors responsible for project implementation, or budgetary allocations for payment of materials and services, as part of the cost of the project. Other legislations also include some indirect expenses, such as part of the current expenditures of the public agencies

TABLE 4.5

Betterment Levy Normative Model: Quotas

Instrument Provisions	Legislation on Betterment Levies	Administrative Directives or Decree Governing Financing of Public Works Through the Betterment Levy
Definitions	Explicit statement that the total revenues will not exceed the cost of the project.	Explicit statement of the cost to be apportioned and its components.
	Broad concept for determination of the amount to be apportioned, with reference to the factors used in the determination and the proportion of that amount to be charged to the levy overall.	
	Explicit statement that each individual owner will pay a quota equivalent to a proportion of the amount to be apportioned, an amount per unit of weight or a percentage thereof, determined according to the circumstances of each case.	Explicit statement of the individual quota or of factors that will be used to calculate it.

participating in planning and supervision of the project. These, however, are not allocated under specific budgetary headings identified with the implementation of the program, the provision for administration of the betterment levy, or, in particular, financing costs.

Different criteria have been applied regarding the portion of the costs to be financed through the betterment levy and that to be covered with ordinary tax revenues. Alternatives encountered range from a 25 percent apportionment up to the total costs incurred. To this effect, it is recommended to adopt flexible criteria under general legal provisions to establish the possibility for participation of all applicable elements in the costs to be apportioned, with inclusion of financing, administration of the system, and aggregate apportionment, while reserving for specific regulations the conditions concerning particular circumstances in specific projects.

Determination of the Individual Liabilities

Once the aggregate has been estimated, it is to be apportioned to the individual properties through a mechanism provided for under the normative provisions in agreement with the system established for determination of the tax base. Whenever the base taken is that of value increases generated in property values, the individual quota will be formed by a portion of the total of this increment. However, when the tax base, instead, is a theoretical value or a distribution factor, the quota will be obtained by dividing the amount to be allocated by the total value.

In any event, it is advisable to specify in the general legal provisions that the individual quota will be the proportion to be paid by each property owner in apportionment of the levy to the tax base and that it be established more specifically by implementation regulations for each project through the establishment of a rate per unit, for example, per square meter or monetary unit of assessed value.

Exemptions

Although it is generally recommended that no exemptions be granted on the levy so as not to detract from its characteristic as a contribution to improvements, some laws provide for exemptions for properties used for public utilities or those belonging to the state or to agencies and institutions normally exempt from taxes, such as churches and educational and welfare institutions.

When it is necessary to grant exemptions, these can be classified under two categories: exemption from being subject to the levy,

TABLE 4.6

Betterment Levy Normative Model: Exemptions

Instrument / Provisions	Legislation on Betterment Levies	Administrative Directives or Decree Governing Financing of Public Works Through the Betterment Levy
Definitions	Specification of exemptions and how they will be granted, either through exemption from the specific levy or exclusion of the property from the benefit area. Authority to designate the procedure to be followed in each case.	Explicit indication of exemptions and procedures for each specific case.

TABLE 4.7

Betterment Levy Normative Model: Deadlines for Payment

Instrument / Provisions	Legislation on Betterment Levies	Administrative Directives or Decree Governing Financing of Public Works Through the Betterment Levy
Definitions	Description of procedures to be followed in each case to set the due dates for payment and statement of the possibility of granting discounts for advance payment or charging interest on deferred payment.	Manner in which the specific levy will be paid; determination of discount or interest charges.

consisting of exclusion of the properties from the differential benefit area, thus apportioning their levy quota among the other taxpayers; and exemption from payment of the levy. In this case, the properties are included in the benefit area but they are released from the obligation of payment of their quota, whereas the state absorbs their non-participation in financing of the project. The selection of either alternative, which is determined by the tax system and traditions of each country, must be explicitly provided for under general legal provisions.

Deadlines for Payment

Normative criteria may also be adopted as concerns the date for payment of betterment levies in accordance with the practices existing in each country and the characteristics of the public works project.

Notification of payment obligations may be issued upon initiation of the project, during its execution, or after its completion.

Collection of the betterment levy should usually be spread over a defined period of time and paid through installments supporting the financial disbursement requirements of the project. The taxpayer may be granted certain options, such as special discounts for early and full payments, interest surcharges for deferral of installments, or postponement of the liability with addition of interest charges when payment is made in a single lump sum.

As was the case with the other points discussed, the general legal provisions are to provide for all options and for a later definition of specific regulations. This aspect is of particular interest because of the relations often existing between implementation of the betterment levy system and the financing of the project. It derives from the link between the resources obtained through loans for the financing of the project, in which case the deadlines for payment and amounts collected have to coincide with the deadlines and amounts agreed for amortization of the loans. This procedure is desirable, at least from a financial and administrative standpoint.

Implementation of the Betterment Levy

Because of the specialized nature of the betterment levy, this study recommends that general legal provisions establish the broad outline of the system, leaving the technical characteristics of each group of public works to regulation through specific implementation decrees or administrative directives. The requirement of making administrative directives conform to a general legal framework

TABLE 4.8

Betterment Levy Normative Model: Implementation of the Levy

Instrument Provisions	Legislation on Betterment Levies	Administrative Directives or Decree Governing Financing of Public Works Through the Betterment Levy
Definitions	Explicit description of the formalities and requirements for specific implementation of the betterment levy and for promulgation of the regulating decree. The regulations must cover: Authorities empowered to impose the betterment levy Participation of property owners Criteria for determining levy subjects, tax bases, and quotas Publication and notification	Description of procedures to be followed after requirements for imposition of the levy have been met.

ensures satisfactory legal protection of individual interests from
arbitrary betterment regulations.

Regulations should expressly provide for the following:

Public authorities authorized to impose a betterment levy: At the
    local government level, executive authority for the implemen-
    tation of the betterment levy normally resides in the ministry
    or agency responsible for the specific project. Tax authorities
    should always participate in the administration of the betterment
    levy.

Representation of property owners: Public acceptance of the better-
    ment levy may be fostered through participation of the property
    owner representatives at the various stages of betterment levy
    implementation, and particularly in decisions concerning project
    approval, determination of the tax base, and prorating of levy
    liabilities.

Definition of criteria for the determination of the betterment levy,
    tax base, and quotas: Betterment legislation should stipulate
    that technical studies be made to propose efficient and equitable
    guidelines for the determination of benefit areas, the portion of
    project costs to be recovered, and the apportionment of the
    betterment levy quotas.

Publication and notification: Procedures with respect to the publication
    of government decisions authorizing betterment projects should
    be formulated. Moreover, property owners should be notified
    of their respective liabilities with sufficient time to allow them
    to exercise their rights to request hearings and legal protection,
    as well as time to resolve objections or to allow for clarification
    of questions that may arise.

IMPLEMENTATION OF A BETTERMENT
LEVY SYSTEM

Flowchart of Activities

Adequate legislation on betterment levies is not enough to
guarantee operation of the system. In many countries, the difficulties
were at the stage of administrative implementation. Important requirements are to attain a reasonable degree of acceptance on the
part of property owners, as well to coordinate the dates of project
programming and implementation with the assessment of liabilities,
and, finally, timely and efficient collections. The process is also to
be related to the negotiation and approval of the loans used for financing of the public works project.

Consequently, the operation of a betterment levy system requires implementation of a series of activities concerning the entire administrative process (programming, integration, coordination, and supervision and control) that are interrelated and linked through an efficient information system. These activities are identified in Table 4.9, and their interrelationships are shown in Figure 4.1.

The activities involved in the implementation of the betterment levy now will be analyzed, with brief reference to concepts and methodologies that have been applied successfully in a number of countries.

Feasibility Studies

While actual implementation of the project and its financing through a betterment levy system must result from an act of government, it cannot be denied that the success of this system is closely connected to the financial capacity of benefited property owners and their acceptance of the project. Consequently, it is desirable to ensure, in some measure, their cooperation. To this effect, it is recommended that a prior survey be made to ascertain acceptance of the project, as well as actual possibilities for collection of the levy from the standpoint of the financial capacity of property owners, overall tax burden, and other relevant factors. Parallel to this, it is necessary to estimate the possible financial contributions that may be made by the different levels of government (local, federal, or central) to evaluate the political and economic feasibility of the project.

Participation of Property Owners

Participation of benefited property owners in project planning and in the assessment of liabilities is a frequently used procedure that has led to satisfactory results. However, in other cases, it has been a serious obstacle to the implementation of projects. The difference exists in the criteria applied to organize taxpayer participation in the process and in the degree of participation granted.

The taxpayers' council should include members who represent owners in the area and who are chosen on the basis of personal prestige, participation in community affairs, or personal abilities as leaders of intermediate groups. Selection of the members to form the taxpayers' council calls for careful decisions on the part of the authorities promoting the project. A common practice is to select leaders of associations of local businessmen, farmers, industrialists, or professionals or, in very homogeneous urban areas, leaders of civic associations or service clubs.

TABLE 4.9

Outline of the Administrative Process

		Stage of the Administrative Process			
Activities		Planning	Inte-gration	Coordi-nation	Control and Supervision
1. General Management					
1.1	Preliminary appraisal	X			
1.2	Study on economic, technical, and political feasibility of the levy and the project	X			
1.3	Passing of decrees		X		
1.4	General supervision				X
2. Engineering					
2.1	Preliminary zone studies	X			
2.2	Preliminary designs and preliminary cost estimates	X			
2.3	Detailed draft project, program, and specifications		X		
2.4	Budget		X		
2.5	Final implementation designs		X		
2.6	Contracting and construction of the project			X	
2.7	Supervision and control				X
2.8	Entry into service of the project			X	
3. Credit—Source of Financing					
3.1	Study of sources of financing and credit terms	X			
3.2	Negotiation of the loan		X		
3.3	Contracting of the loan			X	
3.4	Amortization of the loan			X	
4. Betterment Levy					
4.1	Preliminary survey of taxpayers and estimation of expected range of levy	X			
4.2	Analysis of possibilities for and determination of amounts to be contributed by various levels of government	X			
4.3	Establishment of taxpayer councils		X		
4.4	Definition and general mapping of benefit area		X		
4.5	Detailed mapping and identification of properties		X		
4.6	Detailed demarcation of benefit area		X		
4.7	Socioeconomic studies of benefit area		X		
4.8	Determination of factors and calculation of apportionment tables			X	
4.9	Negotiations with taxpayer councils			X	
4.10	Determination of individual liabilities			X	
4.11	Notification of individual assessments			X	
4.12	Settlement of objections and disputes			X	
4.13	Collection of assessed levies			X	X

FIGURE 4.1

Betterment Levy Flowchart

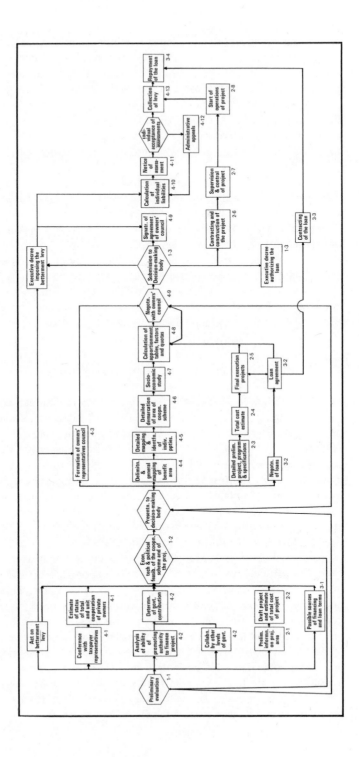

103

The functions of the council, which should be defined under the respective legal provisions, should not go beyond participation in a consultative capacity regarding the evaluation of the public works project, the determination of the benefit area, and the general factors conditioning apportionment of the levy in general terms in the zone or between population groups within the zone. Additionally, property owner representatives may also participate in a supervisory capacity, ensuring that the project is executed in accordance with the approved specifications and design.

In some cases, it has been found that the participation of taxpayer representatives improved initial projects and made their execution feasible. This was because certain sectors agreed beforehand to pay differential value increment quotas to absorb part of the differential benefits that could not be absorbed by relatively less developed zones.

It is, therefore, essential that the authorities involved actively participate in the council and that its work be coordinated and directed by a senior official. The council's decisions should be recorded and reported in formal documents (minutes, resolutions, and so on) and this information should be disseminated to all property owners.

Mapping (Cartographical Studies)

The demarcation of the boundaries of the benefit area and identification of individual properties within it are essential for studies on apportionment of differential benefits and subsequent calculation of individual tax liabilities. There is no doubt that reliable assessment records provide a sound basis for this task. New cadastral systems comprise aerial photogrammetry of the area and complete identification of properties, including dimensions, boundaries, topography, land use and potential productivity indexes, owners' names, and assessed value of improvements. Unfortunately, this information is not available in most countries in Latin America, at least with respect to meeting satisfactory qualitative and quantitative standards.

An alternative solution is to make specific surveys and census of the benefit area with the degree of precision required for betterment levy purposes. The maps prepared for project planning may sometimes furnish a useful basis for the specific land survey. It could be desirable to have these mapping and survey studies used for other tax purposes, for example, by relating them to property tax rolls and records, thus economizing in applicable expenditures. As previously stated, the cost of land surveys may be charged to the project if legal provisions allow it; consequently, the amount expended on surveys can be recovered through the betterment levy itself.

On the basis of a map of the area and detailed analysis of the work program, it is possible to determine precisely the benefit area. In some cases, for example, water supply and sewerage systems, identification of the benefit area may be made very precisely. In others, the problem can be more complex, as with roads or major urban development projects. In these cases, topographic criteria or road-use analyses are usually applied.

Sometimes it may be advisable to introduce economic or administrative criteria to make betterment levy financing feasible. A larger area permits a larger spillover of benefits and consequently lower individual assessments. In all such cases, the only restriction is the possibility of identifying the differential benefits. To this effect, some modifications may be introduced in the original project in order to expand the benefit radius of the central project. For example, one such modification could be to add an access spur to an important road, linking it to a nearby population center that previously was not within the benefit area.

Another important aspect to be taken into consideration is that of differentiation of zones within an area through factors other than location in relation to the project so that the betterment levy may be apportioned with reference to more refined economic criteria. Among these factors a particularly important one is land use.

It is also recommended that socioeconomic studies be made of the benefit area after it has been delimited in order to have information available that may be of use in weighting apportionment of the betterment levy. In the economic field, these studies may range from the income level of inhabitants of the zone to tax burdens and expenditure composition; in a social context, they may range from educational level to tax tradition. Moreover, surveys normally play an important role in promoting taxpayer consciousness and this facilitates imposition of the levy.

Studies of Costs and Quotas

On the basis of the elements derived from mapping and socio-economic studies and of the perfected investment and expenditure budgets for the project, it is possible to determine the factors to be taken into consideration for apportionment of individual liabilities and of the aggregate amount to be apportioned.

The selection of factors from among those mentioned under the normative model, and the quantitative integration of the total amount to be apportioned, form a problem that varies according to the situation, the solution of which must be based on characteristics of the project and the circumstances prevailing in the zone. For this reason, it is important to have sufficient and reliable information available in making prior studies.

An analysis of the different alternatives and the weighting of results in terms of the individual quotas they imply on the basis of sampling process is always useful for negotiation and decision of the quotas to be finally established.

Once a decision has been made on the formula to be used for determination of the liabilities and delimitation of the benefit area, it is necessary, within the applicable legal framework, to issue the regulations providing for betterment levy imposition and for the method to be followed for individual assessments.

Semiofficial Phase of the Tax Process

Individual assessments must be calculated in accordance with the specific regulations issued to this effect. This consists of a computation made by assigning to each property its portion of the total levy on the basis of its individual characteristics as determined in previous studies. A valuable instrument in this procedure is the use of computers, particularly when apportionment comprises a series of different factors that have to be weighted mathematically.

Calculation of individual liabilities will allow the completion of property owner lists for notification and control of collections. Individual liabilities are to be communicated through formal notification so that taxpayers may be guaranteed the right to express their dissent. It is recommended that these assessment notices be issued at the time of initiation of the project and sufficiently in advance of the deadline for payment so that collections may begin on schedule.

The notification should be as explicit as possible so that the taxpayer may receive sufficient information to be able to evaluate the adequacy of his liability. One good method consisted of an assessment notice of the benefit area in map form, showing the factors used for calculation of the liability, the value of each factor as applied to the specific taxpayer, and the payment method and deadline for the same.

Appeals

The types of appeals that may be filed with competent authorities are to be defined by the respective regulations. A good principle is to accept appeals only on the grounds of error on the part of the administration in identification of the property or apportionment of the levy.

An expedient system for the settlement of appeals should be instituted so that these can be resolved as quickly as possible. It is recommended that an administrative unit be set up with the necessary trained personnel and availability of information required for the handling of appeals. This unit should be separate from the normal tax administration processes.

It is equally advisable to limit the deadline for presentation of objections to a short period after receipt of the notification and that property owners be aware that failure to appeal within the deadline represents tacit acceptance of the tax liability assessed. Thus, when collections are initiated, owners will not be able to create obstacles with new appeals and objections.

The timeliness with which levy collection is begun often conditions its effectiveness. This is closely related to the administrative practices and tax education existing in each country. In some cases, collection before the initiation of the project is difficult because of lack of public confidence that the project will be executed. In others, it is more difficult to collect the levy when the project is completed because of decreased interest on the part of taxpayers.

Consequently, this problem is to be resolved in accordance with the specific circumstances existing in each country. Successful experience was observed in some countries where levy collections were systematized through modern and efficient procedures, particularly in cases where the administration of general taxes suffered from a considerable backlog.

The unequivocal fiscal characteristics of the betterment levy and the fact that enforced collection procedures are used facilitate compliance with the obligation to pay as well as effective recovery of the amount owed.

FEASIBILITY OF THE RECOMMENDATIONS

Both the normative model and the recommendations for its implementation reflect the most important and successful experience observed in the operation of the betterment levy system in different countries in Latin America. They also offer solutions for problems found in other countries where the system has encountered certain obstacles.

From the study and analysis of these experiences, it may be inferred that the feasibility of the betterment levy system largely depends on the flexibility of legal provisions in permitting adjustment of the implementation of a specific project to its own requirements. Implementation is difficult for those countries that have a rigid legal tax system requiring that quantification of betterment levy assessments be given in precise terms under pertinent legislation. In the model itself, an alternative was suggested for this type of situation consisting of the inclusion of general provisions of this type in the tax code, or a similar set of provisions, and the passing of specific acts of legislation regulating each betterment levy enforced. It is also possible to explore the possibility of delegating legally the determination of parameters and the assessment of specific liabilities to a consulting firm.

Another factor to be taken into consideration concerning the feasibility of the project is the ability to implement and administer the system. The magnitude of this problem, even in countries that are relatively loaded with backlogs in tax administration, may be limited to the betterment levy itself and may be resolved specifically without having it participate in problems concerning other areas. The authors frequently found specialized agencies created for the administration of the levy—and trained to this effect—handling it with greater efficiency than the general tax administration.

Due consideration is to be given to public confidence in government action as a determining factor of betterment levy system operation. In some cases, lack of receptivity on the part of taxpayers is due to past experiences with levies paid for projects that were never finished, or having been adjusted to original projects, or to promises not kept by the authorities.

Feasibility of the system is somehow conditioned by the type of project. There are precedents of betterment levy financing of projects for transportation, sanitation, improvement of soils, and urban development. For this reason, the model must also be sufficiently flexible to allow for its application to these diverse types of projects. From another point of view, the selection of the project is made on the basis of budgetary and financial considerations to permit execution of some projects in which citizens are specifically interested and that cannot be undertaken with regular fiscal revenues due to formal or financial budgetary limitation. Projects are often selected with original loan financing, since the betterment levy system facilitates this type of financing through the levy yield that provides a guarantee of debt service.

TECHNICAL ASSISTANCE REQUIREMENTS

The limited experience of Latin American countries with the betterment levy system calls for the need to develop a methodology for making cadastral surveys and socioeconomic studies for definition of zones and determination of factors for quantification of individual benefits. The greatest need for technical assistance is in the field of revenue collection of the betterment levy for a specific project, particularly in its implementation and administration—even in countries having a reasonably acceptable cadastre. Technical assistance projects should include collection of cadastral information for the identification of properties whenever necessary, assessed values, feasibility studies, and calculation and documentation of individual liabilities.

In the area of legal provisions, it is felt that the normative model provides guidelines for legal experts in the different countries to make the necessary studies for the formulation of applicable provisions, in accordance with the type of legal system existing in their countries. In some cases it would be desirable to have technical assistance in conducting these studies, particularly as concerns the technical aspects of the betterment levy and the public finance sphere so as to adapt the system to overall fiscal policy.

THE IMPACT OF THE MEASURES PROPOSED

Financing of Investment Budgets

An important aspect should be highlighted regarding the financing of the budget. It is not possible to consider the betterment levy system as a major source of tax revenues similar to income taxes or sales taxes. Its very nature implies that the revenue yield, in the best of cases, will be considerably smaller. Nor can the betterment levy system be thought of as a suitable instrument to finance every type of public investment. Some projects generate such low differential benefits that they do not justify the administrative efforts involved in the application of the betterment levy system. There are even cases of projects generating individual "worsements," which would lead to negative financing or to the granting of a subsidy.

However, financing through this means may be quite significant for some types of public works projects, and there are many cases in which 100 percent of the cost of these projects may be financed through the betterment levy.

The timing of the collection of the levy is very important. If determination, notification, and payment are made on a timely basis, a large part of the levy will be collected at the same time expenditures are made and may cover them directly. In some cases, provided this is permitted by formal accounting provisions, they may even temporarily be used for other projects. If, to the contrary, payment is made after completion of the project, inevitably recourse will have to be made to additional loan financing or to general revenues to bridge the gap.

Certain accounting legislation provides that projects having their own source of financing may be carried out even when no provision was made for their execution in the budget. This is one way of granting these projects a semiprivate status, since whenever the parties interested in the project cover its costs, budgetary controls to a large extent lose their justification. The betterment levy system represents a type of financing that is remarkably well adapted to this self-financing role of certain projects.

Another important advantage offered by the betterment levy, within the scope of the project to which it is applicable, is the fact that it provides a sound financing basis, permitting easier access to all types of domestic and external credit. This is because financing is more likely to materialize and because it provides a debt service guarantee. Monetary correction procedures are an important factor in cases in which inflationary trends are strong and payment of the assessed levy is made in installments over the medium or long term, or whenever payment is made after the due date. This aspect has been discussed in detail elsewhere in this study, and only highlighted here is the fact that in countries where an inflationary trend is present, payment of the levy after assessment always represents a reduced real value.

Infrastructure Projects

To a degree, all countries have a need for a higher level of development in both urban and rural infrastructure. The construction of roads, bridges, urban streets, drainage and sewage systems, irrigation and flood-control systems, and similar projects represents a continuing requirement of public goods or services—suggesting a demand that is never fully satisfied.

This latent demand exists partly because these projects often meet social wants, so that it is the general community that both bene-fits and defrays costs. Only rarely will the individuals that benefit from the projects and the individuals that pay for them be the same people. It is unlikely that the contributions made by the beneficiaries will be commensurate with the benefits received. An important ex-ception is the financing of public works projects on the basis of the benefit principle through user taxes or fees. But there are still in-vestments in many fields where neither system is used.

These comments do not imply a questioning of financing systems based on the ability to pay principle. While these systems have been the subject of much analytic discussion recently, they are undoubtedly closely related to the income distribution objectives inherent in the present value systems of many countries. It should be pointed out, however, that these systems yield projections of a demand for public services that is greater than the demand that would result if the costs were charged to those benefited by the projects. However, it is likely that even if the costs could be charged in this manner, there would still be an unsatisfied demand. This is the case because tax systems have proved incapable of providing the resources required (for reasons that need not be discussed at this time).

The betterment levy system represents an instrument for the financing of public works projects that requires more complex procedures than those commonly used in general revenue-raising operations. It also provides an additional source of financing destined to cover a wide range of public works projects (though not all) of which it can finance a substantial portion or, in some cases, total costs.

The fundamental issue is that the betterment levy offers this contribution to the execution of public works projects without acting to the detriment of resource allocation. It even improves it on the basis of unquestionable equity and particularly of a very specific quid pro quo that obviates the political difficulties customarily encountered with most taxes. The fact that payment of the levy is matched by a real and visible benefit brings this system close to a form of market economy financing normally not hampered by the same disadvantages, such as political resistance, as taxes.

Improvement of Property Tax Administration

There is a close relationship between the betterment levy and property taxes. From the structural standpoint, both of these taxes are imposed on the same taxpayers and use the same tax base, although the causal event generating the betterment levy liability and the parameters for determination of the levy are different. The authors frequently found that a single agency administered both of these tax systems, benefiting from information that may be used in the administration of and in their collection, with significant procedural and cost savings.

From the theoretical standpoint, the data on property tax records form the basis for implementation of the betterment levy through the use of cadastral information identifying and quantifying properties and their owners. In practice, and with few exceptions, these advantages are not realizable due to substantial deficiencies in records or a lack of reliable cadastres.

In some cases, it is argued that lack of information and efficiency of the property tax do not allow for, or largely hamper, implementation of the betterment levy system. It is maintained that, in view of its more general application, priority should be assigned to improvement of the property tax administration instead of the implementation of a specific levy imposed on betterments generated in the area. In other cases, the problem is resolved through ad hoc cadastres and administrative systems specifically established for the implementation of the betterment levy, disregarding any connections with the property tax.

The allocation and yield of the betterment levy for a specific aim serve as a counterargument to the "general" nature of the tax base. Also, advantage should be taken of the improvement of the property tax administration itself, which is easier through a sectoral approach than through a global approach.

Whenever the cadastral information used for property taxes is deficient and specific cadastres are set up for the betterment levy, the information derived from the latter may be used later as feedback for property tax imposition in the area, particularly for taxpayer identification and determination of their tax bases. The methodology used for cadastres and studies concerning the betterment levy may then provide a support for an efficient administration of property taxes, extending its enforcement to other areas and benefiting from the experience and training of the staff who worked on the project.

In any event, assessments made for the determination of the betterment levy base, which already include the increases in value generated by the project, should be used as a basis for the application of property taxes through an updating system that may yield significant revenues from the revenue standpoint. New assessments determined in this fashion also represent a valuable instrument for the administration of capital gains taxes imposed on real estate transactions since they can be used as indicators for the determination or review of income tax liabilities.

CONCLUSION

Three observations remain that are of special significance. First, it is necessary to emphasize the participation of taxpayers or their representatives in the determination of the tax liability. This includes participation in project planning, which tends to show that the levy is based on the benefit principle, and, in particular, guards against errors that when committed frequently may lead to organized opposition.

Second, it is necessary to stress that the sometimes emphatically made suggestion that countries should provide for a betterment levy system as an auxiliary resource for the financing of public works projects does not imply a need to increase the aggregate tax burden. In fact, this is a tax aspect on which it is very difficult to generalize for all countries. There are countries in which the tax burden should be reduced and others in which it should be increased, and there is a third category where it is not necessary to introduce any quantitative changes.

The suggestion to introduce a betterment levy system is not a matter of the level of the tax burden but basically a question of the distribution of that tax burden. It could be maintained that the real estate tax provides the necessary resources, but in this case the tax paid may be levied on both improvements paid for by the owner of the property as well as on those paid for by the community, which leads to inequities in the assessment of the tax. Where the real estate tax does provide the necessary resources, the action recommended is to reduce the rate of the property tax and to add the betterment levy, thus avoiding the situation where all taxpayers pay for the net increases in property values obtained through differential benefit.

Finally, it is necessary to consider the problem of deferred payment of the betterment levy under inflationary conditions. In recent times, lack of price stability has become so widespread that it is difficult to find countries with an annual growth of inflation of less than two digits. There are even countries where the consumer price index has had rates of growth of three digits. This general erosion in the purchasing power of currencies of the different countries suggests the convenience of reviewing a number of issues. Among these is one that is of specific interest to this study involving the liabilities paid long after their determination and notification.

Whenever there is a strong inflationary trend, effectively collected revenues often represent only a fraction of the figure, and are always much lower than the amount of revenue originally projected. Illustrating the importance of this phenomenon, Table 4.10 contains a hypothetical example of a situation in which 80 percent of the cost of the project is to be recovered in a five-year period in a country having a rate of inflation of 50 percent per year. As may be observed in the results in the table, the original goal of recovering 80 percent of the cost of the project from property owners has been eroded to less than 28 percent. In other words, the recovery expressed in nominal terms is 80 percent, but in terms of purchasing power the revenue collected represents less than one third of the 80 percent recovery goal. It is easy to conclude that in a country suffering from high rates of inflation—assuming it is inevitable that collections be made in installments spread over a few years—revenues lose most of their significance in terms of purchasing power.

If a country is trying to set up a formal or informal revolving fund with the revenues derived from the betterment levy to continue implementing projects, it is obvious that under high rates of inflation this fund will nearly disappear in the course of a few years. Although it will show that the projected revenues are being raised in current terms, its purchasing power will gradually decrease until it reaches an insignificant value. If the recovery of the levy is linked to loan payments used for the financing of the project—subject to monetary

TABLE 4.10

Effective Recovery of the Cost of a Project

Year	Nominal Recovery (percent) Cost of the Project	Annual Rate of Inflation (percent)	Accumulated Inflation (percent)	Effective Recovery of Project Costs (percent)
1	16	50	50	10.7
2	16	50	125	7.1
3	16	50	237	4.7
4	16	50	406	3.2
5	16	50	659	2.1
Total	80			27.8

correction or maintenance of value—it will face a shortfall in revenues needed to cover the differences between current values and estimated costs.

Thus, the alternatives are very clear: the levy must be collected in the short term, an alternative not always possible; the state must absorb these shortfalls caused by inflation; or methods must be used to allow for an adjustment of liabilities. Some countries with long-standing experience with inflation, for example, Brazil, have provided for, and apply, monetary correction to this type of debt. Although Brazil has not widely applied the betterment levy, it has used monetary correction for similar types of liabilities and its practical experience merits consideration whenever—as often seems inevitable—payment of the betterment levy is spread over a number of years.

On occasion, an attempt is made to bridge this gap through application of high interest rates, but this is a solution that, in the authors' opinion, is to be rejected because the rate of inflation in a given country cannot adequately be estimated in advance. This is even less appropriate for the longer term. On the other hand, a very high nominal rate of interest could result in an effectively high real rate whenever inflation subsides.

This study does not aim to offer a solution to this problem, but the authors believe it advisable to emphasize the problem so that it may be taken into consideration in the implementation of the system.

NOTE

1. Jorge Macón, "La Financiación del Sector Público Provincial" (Financing of the Public Sector in the Provinces), in La Tributación en Argentina (Taxation in Argentina) (Buenos Aires: Macchi, 1969).

Although the authors have received, through the courtesy of tax authorities in the different countries, extensive information on the legislation in each of the countries used as a basis for this survey, they have not believed it advisable to include this legislation in the study because of its volume. Also, the legislative provisions in various other countries are too diverse to warrant a review of their formal legal aspects within this context. Consequently, it is believed that a description of the essential aspects concerning national experiences with betterment levies suffices as an example for the formulation of the required legal provisions, together with the experiences regarding other taxes existing in these countries. However, a guide to the legislation reviewed is presented below to facilitate the identification and access to this legislation.

Argentina

Decree-Law No. 505/58.

Province of Buenos Aires, Act 7943/72 and Decree 922/73. Ministry of Public Works, Library and Publications Division, La Plata, Argentina, March 1973.

Province of Mendoza, Act 2508/58. Resolution 510/60 of the Department of Irrigation. Decree 3431/64. Decree 4398/65. Act 3603/69.

Bolivia

Municipal Ordinance on the Tariffs Applicable to Remunerated Services in 1973, Heading 50.04.

Brazil

Constitution of Brazil, as amended in 1969, Article 18 II, Brazilian Institute of Municipal Administration, Rio de Janeiro, 1969. Act 5172, Article 81.

Decree-Law 195/67.

Brazilian Institute of Municipal Administration, Model of Municipal Tax Code, Rio de Janeiro, 1974, Articles 250-283.

Colombia

Provisions on Value Appreciation, Ministry of Public Works, National Department of Value Appreciation, Bogotá, October 1970.

Urban Development Institute of the Municipality of the Special District of Bogotá, Value Appreciation Statute.

Provisions of Value Appreciation, Municipality of Medellín, 1970.

Draft Statute on the National Value Appreciation Levies, Republic of Colombia, Ministry of Public Works, 1966.

116

Dominican Republic
   Act 1849/48.
   Act 115/75.
Ecuador
   Act 908/70.
   Decree 066/71.
   Provincial Government System Act, Articles 95 through 108. Pro-
      vincial Council of Pichincha, Quito, December 1972.
   Municipal Government System Act, codified, Articles 415 through
      442, Municipality of Quito, 1973. Ordinance 1386/71 of the Mu-
      nicipality of Quito.
Guatemala
   Municipal Code of the Municipality of Guatemala, Article 98.
   Betterment Levy Regulations of the Municipality of Guatemala City,
      July 30, 1970.
Mexico
   Tax Code of the State of Mexico.
   Cooperation in Public Works Act, State of Mexico.
Panama
   Decree-Law 28/59.
   Act 98/61.
   Act 5/74.
   Act 190/73.
   Decree-Law 20/59 as amended by Cabinet Decrees 15/69 and 17/70.
   Act 1/53.
Uruguay
   Decree 15706/72 of the Municipality of Montevideo, Article 206.
Venezuela
   Expropriations of Public or Social Interest Act, 1947.
   Utilization of National Public Works Act, 1954.
   Draft bill authorizing the establishment of a special levy to finance
      the Caracas Metro, Ministry of Public Works, Ministerial Office
      of Transportation.

A case study to illustrate the practical application of a betterment levy system has been selected for inclusion in this study. It
involves the financing of a highway construction project in Mexico, the
Toluca-Lerma traffic corridor, implemented by the government of
the state of Mexico. In the Spanish original of this study, two other
case studies are included. One involves the master plan for the sewer
system of the central part of Bogotá and the other, the construction of
the Cali-Yumbo and Eastern expressways in the Valle of the Cauca,
also in Colombia. To the reader who wishes to familiarize himself
further with the implementation methodology of the betterment levies,
the study of these additional cases is recommended.

These cases have been selected because they represent some
of the most valuable experiences observed. They allow for clear
identification of the methodology followed in the application of betterment levy systems and illustrate procedures adequate for projects
involving a certain degree of complexity.

The following case has been presented as objectively as possible,
using for this purpose the documents prepared by the authorities responsible for the project. The authors are grateful to the authorities
of the state of Mexico for having permitted publication of these documents, particularly to Professor Carlos Hank González and to Melchor
Rodríguez Caballero and associates, as well as to the advisory team
who participated in the project.

1. PROJECT DESCRIPTION

1.1 Project

The project prepared and furnished by the Communications and
Public Works Directorate for the purposes of this study includes the
following elements:

a) Paved side lanes for low-speed traffic
b) Paved side paths for bicycles
c) Central lanes, which will not be repaved, for unimpeded
   high-speed traffic
d) Median strip, landscaped, including watering system

TABLE B.1

Construction Budget Used for the Study
(thousands of Mexican pesos)

Item No.	Designation	Amount
1	Earthworks	6,233
2	Drainage	10,871
3	Paving	9,703
4	Landscaping	3,000
5	Well drilling	1,800
6	Watering system	2,800
7	Lighting system	8,789
8	Grade separations	4,000
9	Curbs and sidewalks	2,881
10	Bicycle paths	1,000
11	Project studies and supervision	4,828
12	Compensation payments	5,500
13	Contingencies	3,000
Total		64,405

Note: For further details, see Table B.5.

e) Drainage system for collecting waste and storm waters from the lateral areas and the city of Toluca
f) Four grade separations for cross traffic
g) Lighting system for side and central lanes
h) Construction specifications
i) Construction budget (see Table B.1)

2. AREAS BENEFITED BY THE PROJECT

2.1 Criteria for Determining Benefit Areas

The criteria used to determine areas for the appointment of the costs of the works planned are as follows:

a) Magnitude of the benefits that the different parts of the works will generate for subareas
b) Probability of urban or industrial development generated by the works

    c) Length and physical characteristics of approaches to the
       corridor
    d) Natural obstacles (Lerma River)
    e) Effects of other highways (Toluca–Naucalpan, Toluca Belt
       Highway, Toluca–Ixtapan de la Sal Highway)

2.2 Benefit Areas Considered

Map B.1 shows the areas for the assessment, delimited in accordance with the criteria indicated in Section 1.1, after a detailed field and engineering study. In this study, the areas were classified according to the following two factors:

    a) Proximity to the corridor
       a1) Zone A—adjacent to the highway and receiving the maxi-
          mum benefits from it
       a2) Zone B—that area after subtracting Zone A
    b) Kind of area
       b1) Industrial areas
       b2) Residential areas* (see Instructions on Property Valuation
          in the State of Mexico)
       b3) Semirural areas
       b4) Agricultural areas
       b5) Suburban communities

The classification of these areas is illustrated in Map B.1.

3. CATEGORIZATION OF THE SPILLOVER BENEFIT AREA

3.1 Categorization of the Benefit Area by Subarea

Using Map B.1, the total surface of each of the subareas was determined. These surface subareas are recorded in Table B.2. Table B.3 gives each subarea a percentage of the total surface of the benefit area. As may be seen in this table, suburban community and agricultural zones represent 59.30 percent of the total.

----

*Categories: b2.1 Good; b2.2 Average; b2.3 Low Income.

MAP B.1

Toluca-Lerma Traffic Corridor, Mexico

CONVENTIONAL SIGNS

P Industrial Zone Area
R Residential Zone Area
S Semi-Rural Zone Area
A Agriculture Zone Area
E Suburban Communal Area

1 to 22 Toluca Cadastral Units
        Delimitation of zones
        with similar uses but
        different values.
        Paved Roads
        Dirt Roads
        Zone A
        Zone B

121

TABLE B.2

Categorization of the Assessment Area by Subareas
(Mexican pesos)

| | Assessment Subarea | | | Total Assessment Area | |
	Toluca–Lerma	Zone A	Zone B	Square Meters	Percent
Industrial		6,723,450		6,723,450	9.00
Residential	9,512,060	2,012,900	1,318,100	12,843,060	17.20
Semirural		3,788,000	7,080,000	10,868,000	14.50
Agricultural	171,000		28,338,500	28,509,500	38.00
Suburban communities			15,888,370	15,388,370	21.30
Total	9,683,060	12,524,350	52,624,970	74,832,380	100.00

Note: This table for determination of benefit area.

TABLE B.3

Categorization of the Assessment Area by Usable Land Values
(thousands of Mexican pesos)

| | Value of Benefited Land | | | Total Value of | |
	Toluca–Lerma	Zone A	Zone B	Benefited Land	Percent
Industrial		939,942		939,942	26.37
Residential	2,016,095	348,873	19,880	2,364,968	66.33
Semirural		223,620		243,500	6.83
Agricultural	128		16,646	16,774	0.47
Total	2,016,223	1,512,435	36,526	3,565,184	100.00

Note: This table for determination of benefit area.

TABLE B.4

Comparative Summary of the Categorization of the
Benefit Area by Subareas and Value
(percent)

	Usable Subarea	Value of Land
Industrial	9.00	26.37
Residential	17.20	66.33
Semirural	14.50	6.83
Agricultural	38.00	0.47
Suburban communities	21.30	
Total	100.00	100.00

Note: This table for determination of benefit area.

3.2 Categorization of the Benefit Area by
Usable Land Values

To determine the value of the land in each subarea, the following
procedure was adopted: (a) the average unit value of the land (excluding
buildings or installations) was ascertained; (b) the usable land within
each area was estimated as a percentage of the total land area (including all areas); (c) using the percentage derived from (b), the
usable land was determined for each area; (d) the average value of
the usable land in each subarea was obtained by multiplying the usable
value obtained in (c) by average unit value ascertained in (a). The
values obtained are given in Table B.2.

Table B.4 gives the value of the land in each area as a percentage
of the total land value. As may be seen, the agricultural areas represent 0.47 percent of the total value.

Remarks: Area values appearing in Table B.2 are used to
calculate the assessment of each benefit area. These values may not
necessarily coincide with market values of land in those areas.

4. ANALYSIS OF FINANCING COST

4.1 Interest Rate

Bearing in mind present market conditions, the interest rate used
for the study was 13.78 percent per year on the semiannual unpaid
balances.

4.2 Financing Cost of the Works for an Amortization Period of 10 Years

On the basis of the cost of the works estimated in the budget appearing in Section 1.2, the interest rate of 13.78 percent per year on the semiannual unpaid balances and an amortization period of 10 years, the financing cost is as follows:

Financing cost: $64,405,000.00 \times 0.72345 = 46,593,797.25$

5. TOTAL COST OF BENEFIT AREA ASSESSMENT

The total costs for the assessment of the benefit area are included in the following table:

Area	Cost of the Works	Financing Cost	Total Cost
Toluca and Lerma	$12,776,004.00	$9,242,800.10	$22,018,804.10
Zone A	42,816,906.00	30,975,890.64	73,792,796.64
Zone B	8,812,090.00	6,375,106.51	15,187,196.51
Total	$64,405,000.00	$46,593,797.25	$110,998,797.25

6. ASSESSMENT FACTORS

To determine the apportionment of the cost of the works to the different areas, the following considerations were taken into account.

6.1 Factor Representing the Benefits Generated by the Works for Each Area

This factor provides a relative measure of the benefits that each portion of the works will probably generate for each area, according to its location and to the services that it will receive from that portion of the works. Charts B.1 through B.9 give the benefit factors, expressed in percentages and as assigned to each area for each portion of the works.

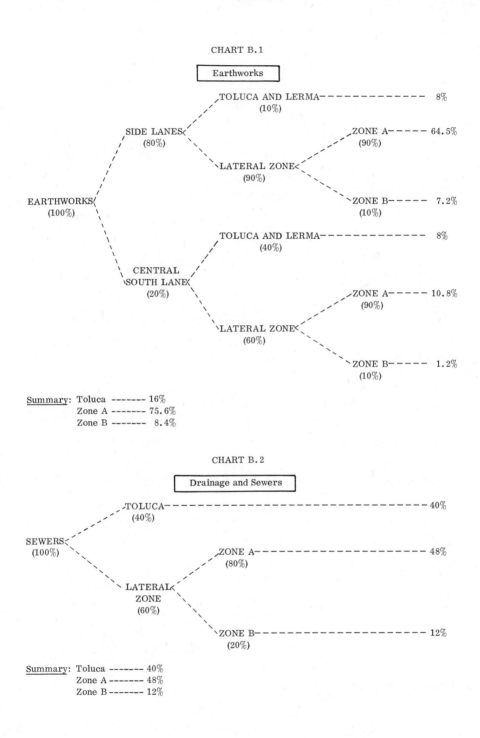

CHART B.1

Earthworks

TOLUCA AND LERMA ------------- 8%
(10%)

SIDE LANES
(80%)

ZONE A ---- 64.5%
(90%)

LATERAL ZONE
(90%)

ZONE B ---- 7.2%
(10%)

EARTHWORKS
(100%)

TOLUCA AND LERMA ------------- 8%
(40%)

CENTRAL
SOUTH LANE
(20%)

ZONE A ---- 10.8%
(90%)

LATERAL ZONE
(60%)

ZONE B ---- 1.2%
(10%)

Summary: Toluca ------- 16%
Zone A ------- 75.6%
Zone B ------- 8.4%

CHART B.2

Drainage and Sewers

TOLUCA ------------------------- 40%
(40%)

SEWERS
(100%)

ZONE A ------------------- 48%
(80%)

LATERAL
ZONE
(60%)

ZONE B ------------------- 12%
(20%)

Summary: Toluca ------- 40%
Zone A ------- 48%
Zone B ------- 12%

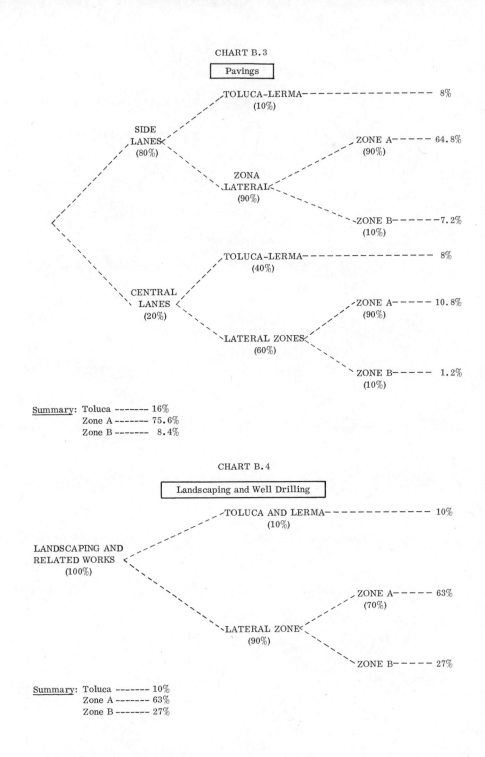

CHART B.3

Pavings

TOLUCA-LERMA -------------------- 8%
(10%)

SIDE
LANES
(80%)

ZONE A ----- 64.8%
(90%)

ZONA
LATERAL
(90%)

ZONE B ----- 7.2%
(10%)

TOLUCA-LERMA -------------------- 8%
(40%)

CENTRAL
LANES
(20%)

ZONE A ----- 10.8%
(90%)

LATERAL ZONES
(60%)

ZONE B ----- 1.2%
(10%)

Summary: Toluca ------- 16%
         Zone A ------- 75.6%
         Zone B ------- 8.4%

CHART B.4

Landscaping and Well Drilling

TOLUCA AND LERMA -------------- 10%
(10%)

LANDSCAPING AND
RELATED WORKS
(100%)

ZONE A ----- 63%
(70%)

LATERAL ZONE
(90%)

ZONE B ----- 27%

Summary: Toluca ------- 10%
         Zone A ------- 63%
         Zone B ------- 27%

126

CHART B.5

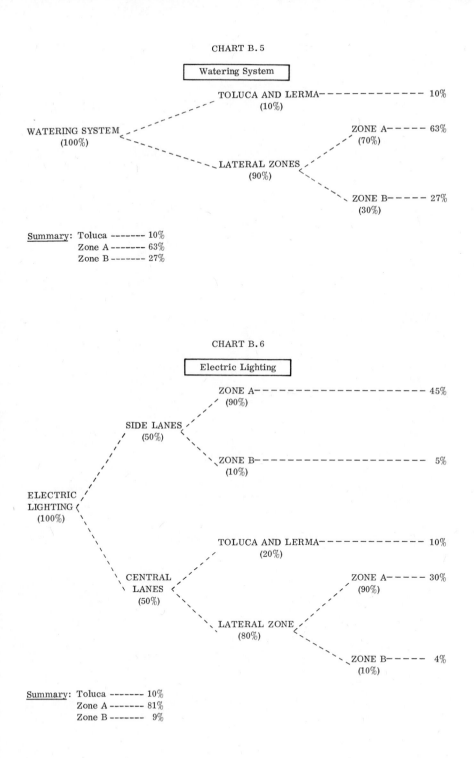

Summary: Toluca ------- 10%
Zone A ------- 63%
Zone B ------- 27%

CHART B.6

Summary: Toluca ------- 10%
Zone A ------- 81%
Zone B ------- 9%

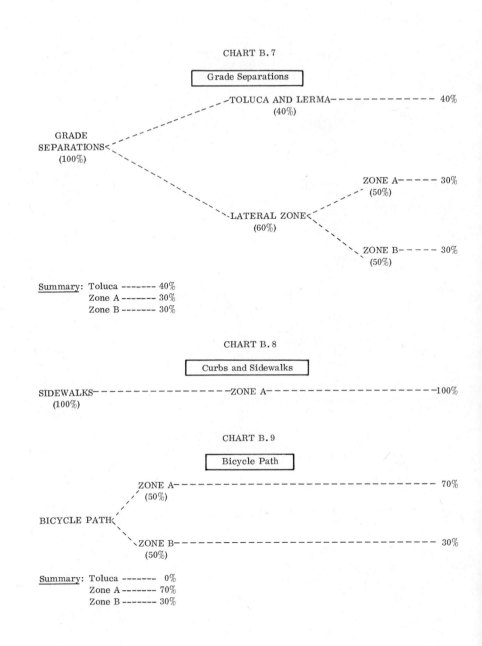

CHART B.7

Grade Separations

GRADE
SEPARATIONS
(100%)

TOLUCA AND LERMA — — — — — — — — — — — 40%
(40%)

LATERAL ZONE
(60%)

ZONE A — — — — 30%
(50%)

ZONE B — — — — 30%
(50%)

Summary: Toluca ------- 40%
Zone A ------- 30%
Zone B ------- 30%

CHART B.8

Curbs and Sidewalks

SIDEWALKS — — — — — — — — — — — — — — ZONE A — — — — — — — — — — — — — — — — — 100%
(100%)

CHART B.9

Bicycle Path

BICYCLE PATH

ZONE A — 70%
(50%)

ZONE B — 30%
(50%)

Summary: Toluca ------- 0%
Zone A ------- 70%
Zone B ------- 30%

128

6.2 Ability to Pay Factor

This factor considers the relative average ability to pay of property owners in each area, and is determined on the basis of the use they make of the land and of the standard of living predominating in the area. The following ability to pay factors were used:

Area	Factor
Industrial	2.00
Residential	
Good	1.25
Average	1.00
Low income	0.75
Semirural	0.50
Agricultural	0.50

6.3 Probability of Payment Factor

This factor considers the relative probability of payment by property owners of their respective assessments. It is determined on the basis of the possibility of locating the owners of the land in the area and by the payment record of the property owners. The following probability of payment factors were used:

Area	Factor
Industrial	1.00
Residential	
Good	1.00
Average	1.00
Low income	0.75
Semirural	0.50
Agricultural	0.50

TABLE B.5

Contributions to Cost Under Budgetary Headings
(Mexican pesos)

Item	Urban Zone Toluca–Lerma			Traffic Corridor Zone Zone A		Zone B	
	Amount	Assessment Percent	Assessment Amount	Assessment Percent	Assessment Amount	Assessment Percent	Assessment Amount
Earthworks	6,233,000	16.00	997,280	75.60	7,712,148	8.40	523,572
Sewers	10,871,000	40.00	4,348,400	48.00	5,218,080	12.00	1,304,520
Paving	9,703,000	16.00	1,552,480	75.60	7,335,468	8.40	815,052
Landscaping	3,000,000	10.00	300,000	63.00	1,899,000	27.00	810,000
Well drilling	1,800,000	10.00	180,000	63.00	1,134,000	27.00	486,060
Watering system	2,800,000	10.00	280,000	63.00	1,764,000	27.00	756,000
Lighting	8,789,000	10.00	878,900	81.00	7,119,090	9.00	791,010
Grade separations	4,000,000	40.00	1,600,000	30.00	1,200,000	30.00	1,200,000
Curbs and sidewalks	2,881,000			100.00	2,881,000		
Bicycle path	1,000,000			70.00	700,000	30.00	300,000
Subtotal	51,077,000		10,137,030		33,953,786		6,986,154
Project study and supervision	4,828,000	19.80	955,944	66.50	3,210,620	13.70	661,436
Compensation payments	5,500,000	19.80	1,089,000	66.50	3,657,500	13.70	753,500
Contingencies	3,000,000	19.80	594,000	66.50	1,995,000	13.70	411,000
Total	64,405,000		12,776,004		42,816,906		8,812,090

Note: This table for determination of benefit area.

TABLE B.6

Assessment Factors

Assessments for Payment in Cash

Zone A $\dfrac{42,816,906}{1,512,435,000} = 0.0283$

Zone B $\dfrac{8,812,090}{36,526,000} = 0.24$

Assessments for Payment Over a 10-Year Period

Zone A $\dfrac{73,792,796.64}{1,512,435,000.00} = 0.0487$

Zone B $\dfrac{15,187,196.51}{36,526,000.00} = 0.4157$

Note: This table for determination of benefit area.

6.4 Tax Benefit Factor

This factor is equal to 1.42. It was established taking into account the fact that the Income Tax Act permits corporations to deduct 42 percent of the assessments paid. In this study, the factor was only applied to areas in which industries were already established.

7. APPORTIONMENT OF THE TOTAL COST
OF THE WORKS

7.1 The apportionment of the total cost of the works given under Section 5 was computed as follows:

a) The value of the usable area within each cadastral unit (colonia cadastral), delimited in accordance with Section 2.2, was determined.
b) The unit value of land within each cadastral unit was determined as indicated under Sections 6.2, 6.3, and 6.4.
c) Total value of land in the cadastral units was determined for each of the areas.
d) The value of each portion of the project budget for each area was determined by applying the factor given under Section 6.1 to that value. Table B.5 gives the results obtained.
e) The assessment ratio for each area for an amortization period of 10 years was determined by dividing the total value of the works for that area by the total value of land in it. Table B.6 gives the results obtained.
f) To determine the average total assessment per square meter of the cadastral unit for an amortization period of 10 years, the applicable assessment ratio was multiplied by the average value per square meter of land within each cadastral unit.

ARGENTINA

Arnaldo Cisilino, Director General, Office of Income Taxes of the Province of Buenos Aires, La Plata

Santiago L. Ferrer, Deputy Secretary, Treasury of the Province of Mendoza, Mendoza

Germinal O. Grandi, Director, Highway Department of the Province of Buenos Aires, La Plata

Juan C. Laurenz, Economic Secretary, Municipality of Buenos Aires, Buenos Aires

L. Ringuelet, Director of Surveying (Ordenamiento Territorial), Province of Buenos Aires, La Plata

Ministry of Public Works and Services, Directors and Staff of the Department of Sanitation, Department of Water Works, Office of Irrigation, Highway Department and Department of Land Records, Mendoza

Carlos A. Vatuone, Deputy Secretary, Economics of the Municipality of Buenos Aires, Buenos Aires

Luis Vernieri Lopez, Consultant (Ordenamiento Territorial), Office of Surveys of the Province of Buenos Aires, La Plata

BOLIVIA

Alfonso Balderrama, Director, Servicio Nacional de Caminos (National Roads Service), La Paz

Eduardo Irahola, Chief of Operations, Servicio Nacional de Caminos (National Roads Service), La Paz

Ruben Mercado, Director, Finance Department, Servicio Nacional de Caminos (National Road Service), La Paz

Daniel Oroza, Chief, Tax Division, Instituto Nacional de Financiamiento Externo (National Institute of External Finance), La Paz

Eulalio Orozco, Deputy Director, Finance Department, Municipality,
La Paz

Mario Paton, Consultant, Instituto Nacional de Financiamiento Externo
(National Institute of External Finance), La Paz

Guillermo Sanjines, Director, Urban Development, La Paz

Carlos Vargas, Deputy Chief, Instituto Nacional de Financiamiento
Externo (National Institute of External Finance), La Paz

BRAZIL

Werner Grau, Deputy Director, Escola Interamericana de Administração Pública (Interamerican School of Public Administration)

Roberto Gomes Moretson, Deputy Attorney General, Departemento
Nacional Estradas de Rodagen, Rio de Janeiro

Cledoaldo Pinto Filho, Manager, Instituto Brasileiro de Administração
Municipal (Brazilian Institute of Municipal Administration), Rio de
Janeiro

COLOMBIA

Luis Arevalo, Secretary General, Instituto Geográfico "Agustin
Codazzi," Bogotá

Raul Gonzalez Perez, Director, Departamento de Valorización de la
Municipalidad (Department of Assessments of the Municipality of
Medellín), Medellín, Colombia

Miguel Gutierrez Navarro, Director, División de Catastro del
Distrito Especial (Land Records), Bogotá

Luis Carlos Hani Abugattas, Chief, División Contribuciones (Betterment Levy Division), Instituto de Desarrollo Urbano (Institute of
Urban Development), Bogotá

Ivan Jaramillo, Director, Catastro del Municipio de Medellín (Municipal Land Records), Medellín

Edgar Osorio Fortuna, Secretary General, División Catastro del Distrito Especial (Land Records), Bogotá

Alvaro Restrepo Toro, Consultant on Betterment Levies, Bogotá

Gladys de Valderrama, National Director of Assessments (Valorización), Bogotá

Rodrigo Velazquez B., Chief, División Factorización del Departamento de Valorización (Factorizatión Division, Department of Assessments), Bogotá

DOMINICAN REPUBLIC

Freddy Bordas, Director, Internal Revenue, Ministry of Finance, Santo Domingo

Carmen Bello de Gonzalez, Chief, Division of Public Finance, Central Bank of the Dominican Republic, Santo Domingo

Maximo Hernandez Ortega, Senior Advisor, Ministry of Finance, Division of Economic Studies, Santo Domingo

José A. Quezada T., Administrative Secretary, Office of the President of the Republic, Santo Domingo

Carlos J. Seliman, Minister of Finance, Santo Domingo

ECUADOR

Guillermo Dahik, Director General of Income Taxes, Quito

M. Garrido, Advisor, Oficina Nacional de Avaluós y Catastro (Assessments and Land Records), Quito

Galo Guarderas Salvador, Director, Oficina Nacional de Avaluós y Catastro (Assessments and Land Records), Quito

Alvaro Perez Intriago, Governor, Province of Pichincha, Quito

M. Ramiro Rodriguez, Deputy Director, Oficina Nacional de Avalúos y Catastro (Assessments and Land Records), Quito

Marcelo E. Yrigoyen J., Director, Departamento de Avalúos y Catastro (Assessments and Land Records), Municipality of Quito, Quito

GUATEMALA

Anibal de Leon M., Director General of Financial Studies, Ministry of Public Finance, Guatemala

Eduardo McCambell, Ministry of Public Finance, Guatemala City

Danilo Cruz Morales, Guatemala City

MEXICO

Horst Karl Dobner, Director of Land Records, Government of the State of Mexico, Toluca

Carlos Hank González, Governor, State of Mexico, Toluca

Melchor Rodriguez Caballero, Advisor, Government of the State of Mexico, Toluca

PANAMA

Luis A. Barria, Chief, Legal Department, National Institute of Water and Drainage Works, Panama City

Francisco Fong, Acting Director, Department of Assessments, Ministry of Housing, Panama City

Edison Gnazzo, Technical Director, Centro Interamericano de Administradores Tributarios (Inter-American Center of Tax Administrators), Panama City

J. Menalco Solis, Executive Secretary, Centro Interamericano de Administradores Tributarios (Inter-American Center of Tax Administrators), Panama City

UNITED STATES

Adonfo Atchabahian, Director, Office of Public Finance, Organization of American States, Washington, D. C. 20006

Richard Bird, Chief, Tax Policy Division, Fiscal Affairs Department, International Monetary Fund, Washington, D. C. 20431

William M. Feldman, Latin American Bureau, Agency for International Development, Washington, D. C. 20520

Ved P. Gandhi, Division of Public Finance, International Bank for Reconstruction and Development, Washington, D. C. 20433

Peter S. Griffith, Tax Policy Division, Fiscal Affairs Department, International Monetary Fund, Washington, D. C. 20431

Orville F. Grimes, Jr., Urban and Regional Development Division, International Bank for Reconstruction and Development, Washington, D. C. 20433

George Lent, Advisor, Fiscal Affairs Department, International Monetary Fund, Washington, D. C. 20431

Roger Smith, Fiscal Affairs Department, International Monetary Fund, Washington, D. C. 20431

Vito Tanzi, Deputy Chief, Tax Policy Division, Fiscal Affairs Department, International Monetary Fund, Washington, D. C. 20431

Oktay Yenal, Chief, Division of Public Finance, International Bank for Reconstruction and Development, Washington, D. C. 20433

URUGUAY

Carlos Garbarino, Accountant General, Municipality of Montevideo, Montevideo

VENEZUELA

Aura Marina Alvarez, Director, Catastro Municipal (Municipal Land Records) of the Federal District, Caracas

Napoleon Antunez, Chief, División de Avalúos (Division of Assess-ments), Ministry of Public Works, Caracas

Lopez Cobeña A., Administración de la Renta del Consejo de Petare (Income Tax Administration of Potare), Department of Sucre, State of Sucre

Juan Jacobo Escalona, Executive Director, Asociación Venezolana de Cooperación Intermunicipal (Venezuelan Association of Intermunicipal Cooperation), Caracas

Jaime Parra Perez, Consultant, Subway Project of the City of Caracas, Caracas,

Emilio Ramos de la Rosa, General Counsel, Ministry of Finance, Caracas

Virgilio Tacoronte, General Administrator of Income Taxes, Caracas

Alberto Trujillo Sanoja, General Administrator of Income Taxes of the Municipal Council of the Federal District, Caracas

SELECTED BIBLIOGRAPHY

Accioly, Aristophanes. Contribuição de Melhoria e Valorização Imobiliária. Rio de Janeiro: Financeiras, n.d.

Ataliba, Geraldo. Contribuição de Melhoria e Instrumentos Afins para Financiamento de Obras Rodoviárias. Rio de Janeiro: Instituto De Pesquisa Rodoviária, 1969.

Barbosa Leite, Daltro. Contribuição de Melhoria; Estradas de Rodagem e Valor da Terra. Rio de Janeiro: Autor, 1972.

Bareto, Joao Luiz de Moraes. "Teoría e Prática de Contribuição de Melhoria." Revista de Administração Municipal. Rio de Janeiro, May/June 1969.

Buchner, David. "Contribuciones de Mejoras." In Tratado de Finanzas, vol. 2. Edited by Gerloff and Neumark. Buenos Aires: El Ateneo, 1961, pp. 187 ff.

Centro Interamericano de Administradores Tributarios. "Documentos del V Seminario Técnico." Mimeographed. Panama City, 1971.

Cornick, Philip H. Special Assessments on Municipal Finance. New York, 1926.

Dobner, E.; and Horst, K. Sistema y Procedimientos de la Tasación, Aplicados al Planeamiento de Nuevos Sistemas Catastrales. Toluca: Ediciones Gobierno del Estado de México, 1972.

Forte, Francesco. "La Teoría del Tributi Speciali." Revista de Diritto Finanziario e Scienza delle Finanze (1953), pp. 330 ff.

Haig, Richard M. "The American System of Special Assessments and Its Applicability to Other Countries." Proceedings of the Pan-American Congress, vol. 2. Washington, D.C., 1915-16, pp. 119 ff.

Harris, C. Lowell, "Land Value Increment Taxation: Demise of the British Betterment Levy." National Tax Journal, December 1972.

139

Harris, C. Lowell, ed. Government Spending and Land Values. Madison: University of Wisconsin Press, 1973.

Holland, Daniel M., ed. The Assessment of Land Value. Madison: University of Wisconsin Press, 1970.

Instituto Brasileiro de Administração Municipal. Aplicação da Contribuição de Melhoria as Obras Rodoviárias Federais. Rio de Janeiro, 1971.

Instituto Brasileiro de Administração Municipal. "Simposio Sobre a Contribuição de Melhoria: Relatorio Final." Revista de Administração Municipal (Rio de Janeiro), January-February 1968, pp. 63 ff.

Instituto para el Desarrollo de Antioquia. Manual de Valorización. Medellín, 1974.

International Bank for Reconstruction and Development. "The Use of Special Assessments to Finance Development Projects." Mimeographed. Washington, D.C., 1953.

International Bank for Reconstruction and Development. "Urban Land and Public Policy—Social Appropriation of Betterment." Mimeographed. Washington, D.C., 1974.

International Monetary Fund. "Land Prices and Tax Policy." Mimeographed. Washington, D.C., 1973.

Janaconne, Pasquale. I Tributi Speciali nella Scienza della Finanze e nel Diritto Finanziario Italiano, vol. 47. Turin, Italy: Biblioteca de Scienza Sociali, 1905.

Laris Casillas, Jorge L.; Merino Mañon, José; and López Ochoa, Jorge. Sobre el Impuesto Predial. Toluca: Ediciones Gobierno del Estado de México, 1972.

Lent, George E. The Taxation of Land Value. Staff Papers. Washington, D.C.: International Monetary Fund, 1967.

Llamas Labella, Miguel A. Las Contribuciones Especiales. Bologna, Italy: Real Colegio de Espana, 1973.

Luqui, Juan C. La Contribución Especial de Mejoras en la República Argentina. Rosario, Argentina: Universidad Nacional del Litoral, 1944.

Lynn, Arthur D. J. The Property Tax and Its Administration.
    Madison: University of Wisconsin Press, 1969.

Macon, Jorge. Financiacion Publica por Contribucion de Mejoras.
    Buenos Aires: Consejo Federal De Inversiones, 1972.

Macón, Jorge. "El Financiamiento del Sector Público Provicional."
    In La Tributación en la Argentina. Buenos Aires: Macchi, 1969.

Merino Mañon, José. La Fiscalidad del Suelo y el Desarrollo Urbano.
    Toluca: Ediciones del Gobierno del Estado de México, 1972.

Ministerio de Obras Públicas, Venezuela. Proyecto de Ley que
    Autoriza la Creación de una Contribución Especial para el
    Financiamiento del Metro de Caracas. Caracas, 1974.

Naciones Unidas. Manual de Administración del Impuesto Sobre
    Bienes Raíces. New York: Departaménto de Asuntos Ecóno-
    micos y Sociales, 1969.

Nicoli, Victor F. La Contribución de Mejoras por Caminos Pavi-
    mentados en la Provincia de Santa Fe. Buenos Aires: Imprenta
    Oficial Coronda, 1940.

Organización de Estados Americanos y Banco Interamericano de
    Desarrollo. "La Tributación sobre Plusvalía y Mejoras en
    América Latina." Mimeographed. Washington, D. C.

Page, William H.; and Jones, Paul A. A Treatise on the Law of
    Taxation by Local and Special Assessments. Cincinatti, Ohio,
    1909.

Pichardo, Ignacio. Ensayos sobre Política Fiscal. Toluca: Ediciones
    del Gobierno del Estado de México, 1972.

Restrepo Toro, Alvaro. "Determinación del Monto Distribuíble y de la
    Zona de Influencia en Obras de Valorización." Mimeographed.
    II Seminario de Valorización. Medellín, 1974.

Restrepo Uribe, Jorge. "La Contribución de Valorización y la
    Planeación de Medellín." Mimeographed. II Seminario de
    Valorizacion. Medellín, 1974.

Rhoads, William G., and Bird, Richard M. "Financing Urbanization
    in Developing Countries by Benefit Taxation: A Case Study for
    Colombia." Land Economics 43, no. 4, November 1967.

Rosewater, Victor. Special Assessments: A Study in Municipal
    Finance. Studies in History, Economics and Public Law,
    vol. 2, no. 3. New York: Columbia University, 1893.

Seligman, Edwin R. A. Essays in Taxation. New York: Kelley, 1969.

Sociedad de Tasadores de Venezuela. "Documentos del I Congreso
    Venezolano de Valuación." Mimeographed. Caracas, 1974.

JORGE MACÓN holds a doctorate in economics and is a professor of public finance at the National University of La Plata (Argentina). He is also a consultant in the field of tax policy. Dr. Macón has occupied several high level positions in the Argentine government. In the international field, he has worked as a consultant for the United Nations in Uruguay and the Inter-American Development Bank, involving the research for this book. As a consultant for the Organization of American States, he evaluated its public finance program. Other consultancies involved several national governments, particularly Bolivia and the Dominican Republic.

Dr. Macón's publications include several books, including one on value-added tax, and numerous articles, mainly in the tax field, such as revenue sharing, income taxes, sales taxes, urban taxation, land taxation, and tax administration. He has also presented papers various conferences, including conferences of the International Fiscal Association and the Institut International de Finances Publiques. His unpublished doctoral dissertation is entitled "Price Level and Equity in Income Taxes."

JOSÉ MERINO MAÑON has worked in the Mexican government since 1960 at the national and local levels, both as a consultant and in an executive capacity, primarily in fields related to fiscal problems. He designed and implemented the recent fiscal reform in the state of Mexico, which included the adoption of betterment levies. At present, he is chief administrative officer of the Ministry of National Properties (Patrimonio Nacional).

José Merino is a public accountant, and has been a professor of public finance at the National University of Mexico from 1961 to 1969. His publications include Del Impuesto Predial (About the Land Tax), Ediciones Gobierno del Estado de México, 1970, and Fiscalidad del Suelo (Fiscal Aspects of Land), Ediciones Gobierno del Estado de México, 1971.

THE ECONOMIC DEVELOPMENT OF PANAMA:
The Impact of World Inflation on an Open Economy
                              Robert E. Looney

LAND USE AND THE INTERMEDIATE-SIZE CITY
IN DEVELOPING COUNTRIES: With Case Studies
of Turkey, Brazil, and Malaysia
                              Malcolm D. Rivkin

LATIN AMERICA'S NEW INTERNATIONALISM:
The End of Hemispheric Isolation
                         edited by Roger W. Fontaine and
                         James D. Theberge

MUNICIPAL DEVELOPMENT PROGRAMS IN
LATIN AMERICA: An Intercountry Evaluation
                         Pirie M. Gall, assisted by Jack C.
                         Corbett, Harry C. Carr III, and
                         David J. Padilla, Jr.

TAXATION AND DEVELOPMENT
                         N. T. Wang